C000229427

SONG OF THE NIGHTINGALE

'What threat could a worship leader possibly pose to the military and political might of a powerful African junta? Unwittingly, Helen Berhane became an icon of the struggle between the powerful and the powerless. Her story demonstrates the power of Christian forgiveness and grace even in the most destructive and heartbreaking of environments. Here you find the beauty and significance of a totally surrendered life that is truly compelling. The locked doors of a makeshift prison shipping container could not contain it. Eritrea has consigned itself deservedly to the ranks of being one of the most severe persecutors of the Christian church in contemporary history. This book reminds us that persecution isn't abnormal, but that the absence of persecution is. It is a virtual 21st century edition of the Book of Acts. Of much greater importance is the reality that our persecuted brothers and sisters have so much to teach us about putting Jesus first in our lives.'

Eddie Lyle, Chief Executive, Open Doors UK and Ireland

'Helen Berhane is one of the most remarkable women I have ever met and her inspirational story should be compulsory reading for every Christian in the West. Becoming a Christian in Eritrea, and indeed in many other countries of the world, entails great sacrifice and nobody encapsulates that sacrifice better than Helen.'

Mervyn Thomas, Chief Executive, Christian Solidarity Worldwide

Release International

Through its international network of missions, Release International serves persecuted Christians in thirty countries around the world by supporting pastors and Christian prisoners and their families, supplying Christian literature and Bibles, and working for justice.

Release was inspired by the firsthand experience of persecution by its founder, Pastor Richard Wurmbrand, who was imprisoned and tortured by the Romanian secret police during the Cold War years of the 1950s and 1960s. Release was founded in 1968, when it was known as Mission to the Communist World.

Richard Wurmbrand himself died in February 2001, but his vision and passion to serve persecuted Christians around the world continues in the ministry of Release today.

For further information, please contact Release International, PO Box 54, Orpington, Kent, BR5 9RT. Tel: 01689 823491. Email: info@releaseinternational.org or visit the website www.releaseinternational.org.

SONG OF THE NIGHTINGALE

One woman's dramatic story of faith and persecution in Eritrea

Helen Berhane
with Emma Newrick

voice of persecuted christians

Authentic

First published 2009 by Authentic Media Limited
Reprinted 2010 (3), 2011 (2), 2012, 2013, 2017, 2021, 2023 by Authentic Media
Limited, PO Box 6326, Bletchley, Milton Keynes, MK1 9GG.
authenticmedia.co.uk

British Library Cataloguing in Publication Data
A catalogue record for this book is available from the
British Library

ISBN 978-1-78893-328-5
978-1-85078-920-8 (e-book)

Names in this book have been changed to protect the anonymity
of individuals.

Cover Design by Claire Marshall

I dedicate this book to future generations, who I pray will not face similar trials, as a reminder that freedom should never be taken for granted.

Contents

Acknowledgements

Thanks to Dr Berhane Ashmelash for his skills as interpreter, and to Colin Spence.

Other prisoners and even the guards very often wondered at how happy Christians could be under the most terrible circumstances. We could not be prevented from singing, although we were beaten for this. I imagine that nightingales, too, would sing, even if they knew that after finishing they would be killed for it.

From *Tortured for Christ*, Richard Wurmbrand,
founder of Release International

Prologue

A single candle flickers, its flame barely illuminating the darkness. They never burn for more than two hours after the container door is locked: there is not enough oxygen to keep the flame alive any longer. It will go out soon.

The woman behind me shifts in her sleep and her knees dig painfully into my back. I try to wriggle over to give her more room, but I am already pressed up against another sleeping body. I pull my blanket up higher and curl up as much as I can. Despite the proximity of so many people, it is freezing cold. Condensation drips from the roof and slides down my cheek, and when it moistens my lips I taste rust. The air is thick with a dirty metallic tang, the ever-present stench of the bucket in the corner, and the smell of close-pressed, unwashed bodies.

I peer around, trying to work out where she is, the woman whose mind is gone. There is a dark shape standing by the small window hacked roughly into the side of the container. I stiffen. Sometimes she blocks the opening by stuffing her blanket into it, cutting off our limited supply of fresh air. Other nights she shouts and wails, rocking the container so that none of us can sleep. She is worse now there are more of us: nineteen in a space that can only sleep eighteen. Tonight she is quiet, and it makes me uneasy.

But I am so tired, and so I force my body to relax against the hard floor. Abruptly the candle snuffs out, I close my eyes, and think of my daughter: Please Lord, keep her safe.

The floor creaks. Someone must be getting up and stumbling across the sleepers to the toilet bucket. I try to shut the noise out. Suddenly, without warning, hands close on my neck like a vice. My eyes fly open, but it is too dark to see. Then there is a guttural snarl, and I know that it is her, the mad woman, her fingers tight on my throat. I push myself up but I have no breath to scream, and I am not strong enough to shake her off. So I do the only thing I can do: I bang my free hand on the wall of the container and kick out. All around us prisoners are waking up. One tries to pull her away from me, but now she has one hand on my throat and the other knotted in my hair, yanking it away from my scalp. I gulp down a breath and manage a scream. The other prisoners start to shout too, and bang the sides of the container. There are shouts now coming from outside, and the sound of hurrying feet, the screech of the bolts sliding back and the pop as air rushes into the container, and then the doors are flung wide open.

My eyes burn as torchlight sears across my face, and then a guard is yanking her away from me and beating her about the head and body with his baton. I fall onto all fours, gasping in air. The guards pull her out of the container, and slam the door again. The other women rush to crowd around the tiny window, so small that only one can see out. One does, and whispers, 'They are beating her!' Her voice is low so as not to anger the guards, who do not like us to look out. She risks another glance. 'They have tied her outside.' The others start to lie down again, looking forward to a few hours of sleep before the guards come again to march us to the toilet field.

I lie down too, but my scalp feels as though it is on fire, and I know that I will not sleep tonight. Sometimes I cannot believe that this is my life: these four metal walls, all of us corralled like cattle, the pain, the hunger, the fear. All because of my belief in a God who is risen, who charges me to share my faith with those who do not yet know him, a God who I am forbidden to worship. I think back to a question I have been asked many times over my months in prison: 'Is your faith worth this, Helen?' And as I take a deep breath of the sour air, as my scalp stings, the mad woman rants outside, and the guards continue on their rounds, I whisper the answer: 'Yes.'

1

Early Days

If you had known me as a child growing up in Asmara, in the country of Eritrea, you would have thought that I was the least likely person to end up in prison. I do not have a rebellious nature. I was a quiet child and a calm teenager, probably because I became a Christian at a young age.

I was born in 1974, and grew up in the upstairs flat of a pretty house that had been built by the Italians, back when Eritrea was an Italian colony. My parents, who were both nurses at the large hospital in Asmara, were from the Orthodox tradition, so it was natural that I began attending an Orthodox church near the house when I was still very young, along with the rest of my family. I came to know the Scriptures, and by the age of 8 I thought of myself as a Christian. I do not remember having a 'conversion moment' – it just seemed clear to me that these teachings were true.

When my younger sister was born we moved across town to a larger house that my father built for us, and I joined the Catholic church near the new house. I had always sung, even as a little girl, but the people at the new church encouraged me, and before long I was singing and writing my own songs in church. My faith had deepened by the time I was 14, and I knew that I wanted to dedicate my life to doing God's work.

I made friends with a girl who was also called Helen, and we would pray and fast regularly together. We were already aware that all was not well in Eritrea – we were in conflict with Ethiopia for our independence – and so we spent a lot of time praying for guidance and change for our country. I felt strongly that I would rather die than live an idle life and make no difference to the world.

I came to see singing as part of my ministry, as well as telling people about the gospel. However, I also cared deeply about the sick people I knew in our community, and I devoted a lot of my free time to visiting them. There are still a lot of people in Eritrea who believe in the power of witch doctors to help them recover from illness. The witch doctors write a prayer, or a curse against the sick person's enemies, on a piece of paper and then fold it inside a small metal sheet, wrapped in a scrap of leather. This is then tied around the sick person's neck, with strict instructions that it must not be removed. Many of the people I visited wore these charms, and so I dedicated myself to praying for them and telling them about the gospel. Often after I had prayed for them they removed the charms, and sometimes they would even burn them. I saw this as a clear testament that God was using me to accomplish his work.

Around this time I was baptized, as I wanted to demonstrate that I was serious about my faith. I was looking forward to continuing my ministry, but I believed I was prepared for whatever challenges God had in store for me.

In 1990, not long after my 16th birthday, I came home from school, impatient to work on a song I wanted to finish for Sunday's service.

Our maid, Ruth, passed me on the veranda with a basket of washing in her arms. 'Helen, your mother wants to see you.'

My mother was in the kitchen, preparing a meal. She looked up from her work, and smiled.

'Helen, we have arranged a holiday for you. You are going to Ethiopia, to Addis Ababa.'

I was excited! I had never left Eritrea before. I would be staying with family friends, and I was looking forward to meeting new people and seeing a new city. I went to my room to plan what I would take with me, before I finished my song. I saw the look of apprehension on my mother's face, but I assumed she was just worried because I had never travelled before.

When the time came for me to leave the house and start the journey to Addis, my mother and father were there to see me off. My father nodded approvingly at me, and my mother smiled uncertainly. They exchanged a look, and she moved close to me, smoothing my hair into place.

'Helen, I hope that you will enjoy your time away. You are going to meet someone who is very important to our family, and who will also be very important to you.' Then she told me that I was actually going to Addis to get engaged. My husband-to-be was an older man, a friend of our family, and our marriage would strengthen the bond between our two families.

On my way to Ethiopia, I thought a lot about this. Arranged marriages still happen often in Eritrea, although they are more common in rural areas. Therefore, it was not a strange thing for my parents to have arranged this. Family bonds are very important in our culture, and so a marriage between two people in order to create or maintain a relationship between two families was not unusual. I had never thought much about marriage, but by the time I arrived in Addis I had decided that although it might take time for me to get used to the idea, I was happy to respect my parents' wishes. My main concern was the age difference – my husband-to-be was 36 and I was just 16. I was worried that we wouldn't have anything in common.

In Addis I was met by our friends and, sure enough, I was informed of my engagement. I had just started to get used to the idea, and was enjoying my new surroundings, when my parents arrived unexpectedly. I was delighted to see them, but I couldn't understand why they had come. I had missed them, but I was old enough now to be away on my own, especially if I was soon to be married.

'You didn't have to come too,' I laughed. 'I'm coming back home in a few weeks.'

My father shook his head. 'Helen, we have come for your wedding.'

At first I didn't understand what he meant, and then my mother said, 'You are to be married here, now.'

My mother explained that I would not return to Eritrea with them, to school, but I would live here in Addis with my new husband.

I nodded. I was apprehensive, but I wanted to be a dutiful daughter. So I swallowed my fears, along with the lump in my throat, and prepared for marriage. Still, I wished that I had been given the chance to say goodbye to my school friends.

After our wedding, my husband and I moved into a house in Addis Ababa, where we lived for a year. Then we decided to move back to Asmara. Eva was born in 1994. The country I had left was very different to the one I returned to. Eritrea was now an independent country, run by the Eritrean People's Liberation Front (EPLF), who had fought a thirty-year war to gain power. Everyone was feeling optimistic about the future.

I, too, tried to be optimistic, but it was hard. My marriage was not a happy one.

My husband, who did not share my faith, had lived in Sweden for a while before our marriage. I assumed that now he would be content to remain with us in Eritrea, but our daughter was only six months old when he left to go back to Sweden for a while. At first I was not concerned; after all, my parents helped me to care for Eva, and my husband still came back every so often and would stay with us for a few months. But the gaps between visits became longer until eventually he was away from us for more than a year. When he finally came back he went straight to my father and handed him an envelope. When my father opened it, it contained divorce papers.

I was sad, because I believed that marriage is sacred in the eyes of God. But I had no choice in the matter. I knew that my husband had felt obliged to get married, just as I had, and that we had both been unhappy. Yet I could not regret that it had happened because it gave me my beloved daughter.

When the divorce was finalized, my husband provided some money to help me support myself and Eva. I knew almost immediately what I wanted to do with it. I had been visiting a friend in the affluent southern part of the city, and I had seen a beauty salon for sale. I enjoyed meeting people, and I thought that I would like to make people feel good about themselves. It would also give me a way of helping people in the community, because I could donate some of the profits to a local aid programme and speak to my customers about my faith.

I was now part of an Orthodox church again and was involved in the renewal movement. I was determined to carry on as usual, although I knew there might be some comments made, as divorce is generally frowned on in my culture.

I walked into church that Sunday, smiling and greeting ladies that I knew well. They did not return my greeting, and one deliberately turned her back to me. I sat in my usual place, feeling confused and hurt. After all, I had not made the decision to get married, or the decision to get divorced. No one came to sit with me, and I left as soon as the meeting finished. When I went the week after, I discovered that there had been a midweek prayer meeting that I had not been invited to, and I overheard some of the ladies whispering about another upcoming meeting, but they shushed each other as I approached. Their disapproval made the atmosphere very unpleasant, and although I tried to explain my situation, and then to ignore their behaviour, I began to feel that I was not welcome in church any longer. Many people stopped calling me by name, and began to refer to me simply as 'the Divorcee'.

'Oh look,' they would say. 'Here comes the Divorcee. What does she think she is doing here?'

I was excluded from church meetings, and finally some church members approached me one day to tell me that I should no longer take part in the services. I should not sing, or preach, and they did not want my involvement in any of the church business. They told me, 'A divorcee can have no place in the church.'

I walked home, bitterly hurt, and I did not return to church. I stayed at home and prayed alone in my room, often throughout the night. I missed the fellowship of other Christians, and for a while I was very lonely, but then God gave me the words of a song: no matter how alone I felt, Jesus was on this journey with me, and although other people had rejected me, God would never abandon me. I started to think even more seriously about my faith, and to read and reread the story of Paul in the Bible. I realized that as a Christian, I must be prepared to face far greater suffering than this. Around this time, I read Richard Wurmbrand's book *Tortured for Christ* and I became convinced that God was preparing me to suffer in his name. I knew that I must be ready to serve, even if it should cost me my life.

Time passed. My beauty salon was flourishing, and I began to enjoy my new life. I would talk about my faith as I braided hair and applied make-up with careful strokes. I loved to see young brides smile at their reflections as I made sure they looked beautiful for their weddings. I also appreciated the opportunities to help other people that owning my own business gave me. I met a woman through the local aid programme, which was one of the schemes I donated our profits to. She, too, was a divorcee and thus isolated like me, but she was also HIV positive and struggled to support herself by washing clothes. I felt blessed in comparison, and I was glad to be able to help her, and other mothers like her.

However, the peaceful future that we had hoped and prayed for did not become reality. There was still conflict between Eritrea and Ethiopia concerning the border between the two countries, and our government had continued and reinforced the programme of military service that the previous government had begun. The atmosphere seemed uneasy, and I felt sure that there was a testing time ahead.

It was 1998, and Eva was 4 years old. That year, war with Ethiopia broke out again – a dispute over a border village escalating into full-scale fighting. The conflict was violent, and in the two years that war lasted I lost many good friends. I was grateful that Eva was still a child and too young to be called up. I loved my country and I understood why my people were fighting, but as the death toll rose it seemed that all this bloodshed was a terrible waste of people's lives. More than nineteen thousand Eritreans died; a huge number in a small country such as ours. It seemed as though every day brought the loss of someone I had known. I felt sorry for all involved in the conflict, Eritrean and Ethiopian alike, and I was convinced that God intended something better for us.

I continued to concentrate on my ministry during this time, as I knew that was what God wanted me to do. There was a Full Gospel Church training centre nearby, and so I started a theology course in my spare time. I often travelled to other towns and villages in the countryside around Asmara, to sing and speak in small churches, and I also shared my faith with people I met on the streets and in the salon. Gradually I became known as a singer, and many churches wanted me to visit and sing for them. I was glad that God was using me.

I had met another Christian who was also a singer. His name was Yonas Hail, and we became friends. I was delighted when he told me that he was making an evangelistic film to distribute across Eritrea and that he wanted me to take part in it. Making the film was dangerous for Yonas, because he had been in the army but kept deserting. They usually caught up with him and put him in prison, but every time he was released he escaped again. He was in hiding, having just run away, and he was always very careful to keep to the backstreets when making his way to the house where we were rehearsing. We called the film *The Gospel is the Cure for the Land*. It followed one man's journey to faith, set in Eritrea. We hoped that many people would see it and learn about the gospel and that it would ultimately help to heal our land. The film quickly became popular among young

Eritrean Christians, and we were encouraged when we saw it being used as part of their ministry.

I did not know that my whole life was about to change.

2

Testing Times

It was around 8 o'clock on a Sunday evening, in the early summer of 2000, and I was walking home through Asmara with some friends. I had been leading Bible studies at a house group earlier in the day and I needed to call into the salon so that I could do the accounts. The women who worked with me would need their wages promptly to help them support their young children. It had been a busy day, and as I walked I was thinking longingly of the meal I would prepare when I finally arrived home.

We stopped to get a taxi in the city centre. There is a large Catholic church there, known as the Cathedral to everyone in Asmara. It is at the top of a long flight of steps, by the main road, and many people use it as a place to meet friends, to sit and socialize. Most days you can find groups of teenage girls giggling at the young men who slouch nearby, pretending not to notice them. On the main street, grandmothers catch up on the gossip and older men discuss the day's business. People from all walks of life pass by.

The weather was good that evening, and the steps were crowded with people chatting, laughing and relaxing.

As we reached the taxi stand at the bottom of the steps I looked at the people enjoying themselves, and I felt an overwhelming compassion. The situation with Ethiopia was still unstable, and it was clear that both countries were preparing for a major battle. In a short time, many of these people laughing in the sun might be dead, killed on the warfront. I was convinced in that moment that without intervention from God there would be more bloodshed, and I knew that he wanted me to speak to these people.

I looked round for my friends. One had already spotted someone he knew, one was trying to hail a taxi, and the last man stood near me, just waiting. I pushed my handbag into his hands.

'Hold this for me, I am going to preach.'

I turned and walked up the steps to the top, leaving my bemused friend clutching my things. When I reached the top I stopped and clapped my hands loudly to catch people's attention. I still didn't know exactly what I was going to say, just that God wanted me to reach out to these people, many of whom were now turning towards me curiously.

'We live in a great country,' I said. 'We may be small, but we are determined, and we have much to be proud of. But this war is tearing us apart. We have all lost someone. I myself have lost many good friends in the fighting.' I could see people near me nodding in agreement. I continued, 'And now it seems that there will be more fighting, and more of our brothers and sisters will die. Even some of you here may not have long to live. So I believe that what our country needs now is reconciliation. God does not want to see more of his people die. Didn't Jesus tell us that we should love our neighbours? We must all pray that Eritrea and Ethiopia can find peace, and that this war will end very soon.'

Gradually people moved closer to hear what I was saying, and I saw that some of them were crying, moved by what I had to say.

After a few minutes, I finished speaking and walked down the steps. About halfway down I realized that there were two casually dressed men standing among the crowd at the bottom of the steps, staring fixedly at me. As I stepped on to the road they lunged forward and grabbed me by the shoulders, one on each side of me. My suspicions were confirmed – they were members of the secret police. I was afraid, but I knew that they could not harm me if God did not will it.

They dragged me through the crowd, many of whom were shouting at them to leave me alone.

A man pulled at one of the policemen's arms, asking, 'What has she done? Where are you taking her?'

A woman beside him shook her head. 'She has done nothing wrong. All she did was to speak about Jesus. That is not a crime.'

The policeman just shrugged the man off and kept walking.

When we reached the road, one of the policemen got into a car and drove off. The other started to walk, still holding my arm. Some of the crowd were still following us,

but gradually they fell away until there were just two
people: a man who said he was a journalist, and one of my
friends from the house group who was pretending that he
did not know me, so that they would let him give a state-
ment.

We walked to a young offenders' prison which was nearby.
It was in an old Italian-style building that looked more like a
family home than a prison, with a very small compound, narrow corridors and tiny rooms. The policeman ordered me to
sit in the reception area until the prison chief was called. But
when he came and saw that I was obviously not a young
offender he shrugged, shook his head and refused to admit
me as a prisoner. The policeman was angry but the chief was
adamant, so he was forced to take me on foot to First Police
Station (in Eritrea, police stations have numbers instead of
names).

I had often passed the police station, but this was the
first time I had been inside it. I was taken straight to the
chief policeman's office for questioning. It turned out that
the other secret policeman who had arrested me had gone
ahead by car and made a false report, saying that I had been
speaking against the imprisonment of Eritreans and telling
everyone that the president and government should step
down. He knew that if he had told the truth about what he
had heard – that I had just been preaching the gospel –
then they would have had to let me go.

The chief motioned for both policemen to leave us,
then sat down at his desk and folded his arms across his
blue-uniformed chest. His cap sat on the table beside his
baton, which I thought must be there to scare me. I did

feel nervous, but I knew I had done nothing wrong. As I waited for him to speak, I studied him. He could have been the same age as my father, but he looked older because of the grim lines set in his face.

'Is this true?' he asked. 'Were you preaching against the government?'

I shook my head. 'I only spoke about the gospel, and how sad I was that so many are dying in the war. I am loyal to my country, and only want to see it prosper, and I believe that for that to happen people must have faith in God. I was saying that we should pray for the end of the war.'

The chief then called the journalist to come and give his version of events. The man stood in the office and looked very uncomfortable. 'I am sorry,' he said, 'but I only arrived at the end and I did not hear what she said.' I had seen him there during my speech, but he must have been afraid of what the secret police might do if he told the truth.

The chief scowled at him. 'You are wasting my time,' he said. 'You are supposed to be testifying. How do you expect to do that if you didn't hear or see anything that happened? Go home!'

Then they brought my friend in. He did not mention that he was a Christian, or that he knew me, but simply explained what he had heard me say. At that time the churches were still open, and it was not a crime to speak about Jesus, so the police didn't know what to do with me. They told me to wait outside in reception, and I saw several more police go into the chief's office, obviously to discuss me. I sat and prayed that the Lord's will would be done. If it was his will that I should be freed, then I would be free, and if he wanted me to be imprisoned, then I would be content to suffer for his name. But in the late evening they called me back in, took my name and address and told me to come back the next morning.

In the morning I did not go to the salon as usual. I called my parents and let them know that I had been arrested the night before, in case the police decided to detain me. I wanted to make sure that they and my daughter Eva knew where I had gone, and that someone would be able to sort things out at the salon. Then I went back to First Police Station, and reported to the chief's office. He sat behind his desk and glared at me, just as he had the day before. I was sure that he felt I was wasting his time, and I wondered if he would have been content just to warn me and then let me go. However, because of the report the secret police had made, he was forced to treat me as a serious threat to the government.

He began to fire questions at me. 'Where were you born? Where do you live? Where do you work?'

I told him about myself honestly and in as much detail as I could, but my answers didn't seem to satisfy him. He leant forward across the desk between us. 'Why did you go to our government's historical place to preach? Were you trying to make a point?'

At first I didn't understand what he meant, but then I remembered that the government had renamed the street on which the Cathedral stands 'Independence Avenue' after Eritrea was liberated.

'I was not thinking of it as a historical place,' I said. 'I know it as a church, and I was preaching from the church building and not from the street. I didn't mean anything political by preaching there.'

He shook his head. 'I am giving you an official warning. You must never preach again.'

I knew that he wanted me to meekly agree, but I could not deny my God. I held my head up and retorted, 'I will never stop preaching. The gospel cannot be stopped.'

He was still shaking his head at my defiance. 'You were talking about bloodshed, and about those people who are dying in the war. Why should you be so concerned about it? Are you obsessed with death?' Then he began to tease me, saying, 'I know! You must have had a boyfriend who died in the war.'

In my culture it is very insulting for a man to speak to a woman in this way, but I just calmly told him the truth.

'I am concerned about it because all Eritreans, and all Ethiopians, too, are my brothers and sisters, and I do not want any of them to die.'

An Ethiopian Orthodox priest had recently been on the news, praying for total annihilation of both the armies, and it had made me and my friends very sad. His actions were not Christian and would not help the situation to be resolved. The chief mentioned this man.

'Even priests cannot make any difference to the situation, so why should you try?'

'Priests should speak about reconciliation, not destruction,' I replied. 'God does not want us to kill each other. That man's actions in praying for so many fighters on both sides to die was unworthy of his faith, and it shocked me and my friends. We are not praying for people to die;

instead, we are praying that the war will be over soon, as that will be better for both countries.' We talked about this for a while, and the chief began to look a little more friendly, now that he was sure that my concern was genuine and that I was not trying to overthrow the government.

Eventually, he said, 'Some of your preaching does make sense, Helen, but there is nothing you can do about war. Your preaching may be useful in the future, but now is not the time for it. You are young, and should be enjoying life, not worrying about these things which do not concern you. I will release you today, but you must not preach again.'

I left the police station, but I had no intention of obeying his order. It would not be long before the strength of my conviction was tested again.

3

Arrested!

A week after I was arrested at the Cathedral, I went, as usual, to a house group in the centre of Asmara. I then went on to another gathering where I was booked to sing, which was in a residential part of the city. We began the meeting, and almost immediately there was a battering on the door. The host opened it to find an irate man standing on the step.

'What is all this noise?' he demanded. 'Don't you know people are trying to sleep? Why should we be disturbed by your loud singing?'

The host apologized and asked politely which house the man lived in. He shook his head impatiently. 'I didn't say I lived here. I was passing through and I heard you. You should think of other people.'

The host promised that we would make sure we sang quietly, but pointed out that none of the residents had complained. The man left, still very angry. It was obvious that he was just trying to make trouble. We found out later that he had gone straight to Second Police Station and reported that we were causing a disturbance.

I had just begun to sing for the people, when there was another banging on the door. This time when the host opened it a large group of police shouldered their way in. I saw them spilling into the room, but carried on singing, because I refused to let them stop me worshipping. Incredibly, they waited until I had finished, and it was only when I began my second song that they ordered me to stop and told us all to produce our ID cards.

They took us all to Second Police Station – there were about twenty of us, all adults, a mixture of men and women. When we got to the police station they began to interrogate us. They wanted to know why we had been meeting there. One policeman pointed at me and said, 'That one. She is the leader. Ask her what she was doing there.'

I replied, 'We only gathered there to preach and hear the gospel, and we were not causing any disturbance. It is not a crime to worship God. You should release us, as we have not done anything wrong.'

But they kept us until late into the evening, and many of those with me were getting worried, as the next day was Monday, and if they were kept in prison overnight and did not go to work, they would lose their jobs. Most businesses in Eritrea are run by the government and they are very strict; often, being late to work once may result in the person being sacked. Some people were afraid and upset because they had never been arrested before. We tried to encourage each other, and we prayed, until at last, late that night, the police gave us a strong warning to stop meeting together, and released us. But most of us were resolved to carry on meeting as before.

Even though I had now been arrested twice, I was determined that I would continue my ministry. I often went to the hospital to talk to the sick people and tell them about the gospel. About a month after my second arrest, I went to the hospital as usual. One of the nurses came to greet me and said, 'Helen, he is here again today.'

Everyone in the hospital knew exactly who she meant. There was a man who was well known for coming to the Intensive Care Unit and waiting for people to die, and then buying coffins for them. He was a wealthy businessman who had spent many years in America, and he claimed that he did this out of charity. It was a very odd thing to do though, because there are many poor people in Eritrea, and he could have helped them more effectively by buying medicines for them. The dead do not care whether they have a coffin or not! The nurses had often tried to explain this to him, but he refused to listen, and so most people believed that he was either suffering from some kind of mental illness or that he belonged to one of the 'death cults' – cults that venerate death. The nurses often tried to get him to leave, because he upset the patients and their families who knew he was hanging around waiting for someone to die.

When I heard that he was in the ICU as usual, I went in and started to talk to him about the gospel. But he did not want to listen to me.

He began to yell, 'You have no right to speak to me about that! How dare you humiliate me in front of these people?' He pushed his face close to mine and snarled at me, the spit flying and his eyes almost popping out of his head. I began to worry that he was not completely sane. The nurses were forced to call security and the security guards tried to calm him down.

'She is just a young woman,' one said. 'What harm can she do? You should not shout at her like that.'

But he wouldn't listen, and kept shouting, 'Take her to the police station! She has humiliated me, and I want her arrested.'

He was so angry that the guards decided it would be best if they did call the police. So the police came, and we were bundled into a police car and driven round to Sixth Police Station. I felt quite alarmed by the man's behaviour; he seemed to be so irrationally angry and I was uncomfortable at being so close to him in the car. When we arrived, I was quite relieved to get out. The two policemen who had come to the hospital took us into a small interview room, and the chief policeman asked us why we were there.

'She humiliated me in front of everyone at the hospital,' the man answered. 'I want you to arrest her!' But the policeman had also heard about this man, so he asked him what he did for a living. The man lied, claiming that he was a farmer.

The policeman then asked, reasonably, 'What is a farmer doing in the ICU?'

He shrugged and said that he helped people by buying coffins for them.

I said, 'But if you want to help people, why not buy medicines for them? You must have another motive for buying coffins.'

He lost his temper again and began to shake with anger. The policeman saw that the man was likely to become violent again, so he sent him home, while I was kept at the police station.

The policeman asked me, 'Where does he get the money to buy these coffins?'

'If you are concerned about where he is getting the money, why let him go?' I retorted. 'How should I know where his money comes from? You should ask him this, not me.'

It was obvious that they did not know what to do. They should have arrested him, because his behaviour was causing a disturbance, but it was easier for them to arrest me, as I did not make trouble. So they handcuffed me and put me in a solitary confinement cell.

This was the first time I had truly been in prison, and I forced myself to remain calm, although it was difficult. The cell was very small. It was only just wide enough for me to lie down on the floor. As the door closed behind me I suppressed a cry of panic at being in such an enclosed space. It was very dark, hot and airless. I slid down the wall, sitting with my back against it, but it was hard to find a comfortable position. The metal cuffs held my arms tightly behind my back, and got tighter if I so much as twitched my hands. My fingers quickly began to tingle and sting as the metal bands, and the awkward position I was forced to sit and eventually lie in, cut off my circulation. Very soon I started to feel dizzy, and as I looked at my legs in the dim light, I noticed my skin beginning to peel through dehydration in the heat. That first day seemed to go on forever, and I lost track of time very quickly.

I was in there for twenty-four hours, and I spent the whole night in pain because no one had come to take me to the toilet, and I could not bring myself to just go in my cell. When a guard did finally come to take me to the toilet, he stood outside the toilet door, which did not lock, and kept knocking for me to hurry up. Then he put me back in my cell.

This went on for several days. I was in the cell for twenty-four hours at a time, often without a toilet break. Then a policeman would take me to the office for interrogation. I sat there, my eyes burning with the unaccustomed light, and I struggled not to slide to the ground as my head spun. My family kept bringing me home-cooked food in a metal pan, but the guards always tipped it into a plastic bag and pushed it into my cell, so I had to eat it from the bag with my fingers.

At last, after eleven days, they took me out of my cell and marched me to the courthouse, where the angry man had lodged a case against me.

When I got to court, the man was already there because his neighbour was suing him! She complained that she could not sleep at night or during the day, because he was always disturbing her. When I heard this I became convinced that he had some kind of mental illness. When her case was finished, he brought his case against me. He demanded that I apologize not only in front of the court, and in front of the hospital staff, but that I also apologize in front of the whole congregation at my church, and admit that I had been wrong to tell him about the gospel and to humiliate him. I refused to do this, so they took me back to the police station.

This time, though, they did not put me back in my solitary cell, but put me in a large cell with a group of women. I was so happy to be somewhere light and airy, and I enjoyed the women's company. I began to sing for them, which helped pass the time and kept us cheerful. Later that day, the police took me back to court, but the man still would not compromise on his unreasonable demands, so I asked to speak to the judge in private.

The judge was an elderly man with a calm demeanour, and he listened carefully as I explained what had happened at the hospital and as I told him about myself and my faith. I wanted him to see that I had meant well, and that the man's reaction to what I had said was unreasonable.

When I had finished, the judge said, 'As you seem so keen to help others, perhaps you could give me some advice?' He explained that he had a problem with his wife which was worrying him, so I listened to him and tried to help as best I could. He made no comment about my Christian faith, and I do not know whether he too was a Christian, but when we went back into court he settled the case in my favour. I felt sure that God had been watching over me and had intervened to have me released.

For a while, life in Eritrea was more peaceful, at least on the surface. The war was officially over, but there were still tensions between the two countries, and our government, led by President Afewerki, was becoming stricter and less tolerant; closing the private press and arresting academics and other prominent people who criticized it.

Then in May 2002, the government issued a decree that it would only recognize four faiths in Eritrea: the Orthodox Church, the Catholic Church, Islam and the Lutheran-affiliated Evangelical Church. All other faiths, including long-established, internationally recognized Christian denominations such as Presbyterians, Baptists and Methodists, as well as indigenous evangelical and Pentecostal churches like mine, would need to re-register their churches, and while the registration was processed they would be forbidden to meet at their church buildings. I was a member of Rhema Church, which was a Pentecostal group, and although our church leaders were sad, they trusted that the government would fulfil its promise to reopen the church once we had registered.

However, not only did our government refuse to register the churches, it also began broadcasting anti-church propaganda. It accused Christians of taking bribes from foreign organizations like the CIA, to cause discontent among the people and create a favourable atmosphere for foreign invasion. Soon the government began to arrest people simply for having a Bible, regularly raiding private homes and small meetings, as well as social gatherings among known Christians. It even arrested Christian business owners. Many Christians were arrested for conducting family devotions in their own homes, and people were taken from their beds, from their offices and from the streets.

I was shocked. I loved my country and I had thought that our government wanted what was best for Eritrea, but now I saw that this could not be true. How could it imprison law-abiding, hard-working people simply because of their personal beliefs? The atmosphere in Asmara became really oppressive. Anyone could be a member of the secret police, so it was hard to trust people. A man might come home to discover his wife had been taken away, or a woman might wait in vain for her husband's return from the office.

I was still writing gospel songs, and I was planning to release an album. I threw myself into writing and practising, and I still did some Bible teaching in one of the Orthodox churches that had remained open.

Months later, in 2003, my CD was finished. Rhema had gone underground since the church closures, but they were still willing to support me and help to distribute the album. I was delighted that my songs would reach a wider audience and help to spread the gospel. I truly believe that fear and the gospel do not go together, and I was determined that no matter what happened, I would still continue to do God's work.

4

Prison

Shortly after I released my CD, some young people asked me to lead a Bible study class three times a week at one of their houses, and I agreed. We met in the cellar of the house, usually very late at night, in secrecy. I knew it was dangerous, but I was determined to carry out the mission God had given me, so I was prepared to take the risk of being caught and punished.

I had been teaching there for about a month, when I cycled as usual to the meeting. It was after midnight, so I wasn't expecting to see many people on the streets. But, as I was locking up my bike, I overheard two young men talking. They were loitering on the corner of the street in the shadows, and as I passed by, I distinctly heard one of them say, 'She's the one.'

As I walked into the house and started to go down the steps to the cellar, I wondered whether to go ahead with the meeting. I was concerned about what would happen to the young people if we were caught, but as soon as I saw the eager faces of the group, I knew that God wanted me to be there.

That night there were fifteen young adults crowded into the small stone room, including two teenage girls. As I began to tell a Bible story, the cellar door burst open without warning and a horde of secret police barged in. There were too many of them to count, and they filled the cellar, shoving us into the centre of the room. There was a strong smell of alcohol, and I realized that many of the men were drunk. They all held batons, and many also clutched plastic whips. They began to beat us with the batons and whips, and even with their bare hands. Blows rained down on my head and back as I crouched on the stone floor. We pressed together to try to protect the young girls who huddled at the centre of our group, but the police were merciless.

I felt one of the policemen's fingers close on my arm, hard enough to bruise, and he dragged me away from my friends and up the stairs into the house. He walked so fast that I could not get my footing and my shins jarred painfully against the stone steps. The house had been turned upside down, with shelves pulled over and books and CDs spilling across the floor. My captor's boot crushed one loose CD to glinting shards.

As he pushed me out of the door, I saw the landlady huddled in the corner, her eyes full of fear. I heard later that they had burst into the house, shouting, 'Where is the singer? We are going to execute her!' She had bravely replied that she did not know any singer. But they ransacked the house and found two copies of my CD and a DVD of the film that I had made with Yonas. They shook these in her face. 'We will shoot her when we find her!'

Then they searched the house until they found the door to the cellar. The two young men that I had overheard in the street must have told the police where I was, or perhaps they too were secret police.

There was a truck parked outside and my captor dragged me over to my bike. 'Put it on the truck. Now!' he commanded.

My hands trembled as I fitted the key in the lock and unfastened the chain, but I managed to wheel the bike over to the truck and tried to lift it. The truck had high canvas sides, and I saw that I would have to lift the bike over my head in order to get it in. I tried, but it was heavy and I was not strong enough to lift it that high. My arms shook with the effort, and I had to let it drop. I heard the other men coming out of the house behind me, and then I felt a searing pain across the back of my legs. My captor drew back his whip again.

'Hurry up! You are wasting our time.'

The others jeered at me and more blows rained down on me, from my head to my ankles. It did no good: I just couldn't lift the bike. My captor lost patience and heaved it in himself, then shoved me roughly into the truck.

After what seemed like only a few moments we drew up outside Sixth Police Station, and they pushed me into a large cell. There was a female guard on duty, and as I stumbled into the cell she yanked the *gabi* (a traditional white shawl) I was wearing off my shoulders.

'See how you like being cold,' she sneered.

It was now after 2 a.m., and the cell was full of women. A lady in the corner wore a smart dress and high heels, but she was slumped against the wall in what seemed to be a drunken sleep. Beside her were two young girls in grubby and tattered clothing with bare feet, and I guessed that they must be street children. The woman beside me introduced herself.

'I'm Zula,' she smiled, her red-painted lips smudged.

'What are you here for?' I asked her.

'Prostitution,' she shrugged, unabashed. 'What about you?'

I explained what had happened and mentioned that I was a singer, and she clapped her hands in delight. 'Will you sing for us?'

Zula explained that the women in the cell were a mixture of prostitutes, thieves, street girls and bar girls. I sang for all of them.

Every so often the guards came to take me for interrogation. As I walked past the cells there were some prisoners who recognized me from my last arrest, when we had shared a large cell, and they shouted, 'The singer is back! Don't forget to sing for us.'

I had been there almost a week, and I was again singing for the other prisoners, when two guards – a man and a woman – opened the cell door and ordered me to come out. One of the other prisoners, a lady called Almaz, got up and came out with me.

The female guard frowned. 'I called for Helen.'

Almaz replied defiantly, 'Yes, and I am coming with Helen.'

It was late at night and they took us outside and made us kneel in the wet muddy grass. Because the female guard had already taken my shawl away, I was just wearing the T-shirt and jeans I had been arrested in. Although it was May and the warm season, it was still cool at night, and within moments I was shivering. Immediately, Almaz took off the jumper she was wearing and gave it to me. I often found that in prison there was someone who cared for me, and I believe that it was God ensuring that I was not alone.

The female guard bent over and nipped my nose hard between her fingers. She began to pull me around the grass by my nose, hissing, 'Stop singing!' My eyes began to water with the pain.

When she released me, both guards began to interrogate me, wanting to know everything about my family, my home, my job and my beliefs. When I had answered all their questions, they left us outside in the cold. We were there for four hours, kneeling all the time, until they finally took us back to our cell.

The next morning I was sent to the official interrogator. Every prison in Eritrea has one, although guards and prison chiefs can also interrogate. The official interrogator's job is to conduct an initial screening interview. At this stage, the interrogator wants to get as much information as possible from the prisoner, so they are usually very polite. Mine was male, and he was very softly spoken. He wanted to know everything, from where my beauty salon was to my future plans. When he asked about my religious beliefs I told him that I was willing to die for my faith.

After my interrogation they did not return me to my cell. Instead, they took me outside and made me climb onto a military truck with some other prisoners who were being

transferred. I caught the name 'Adi Abeito' and I was horrified. Adi Abeito is a well-known military prison, reserved
for soldiers and military personnel. Why would they
imprison me, a civilian, there?

We jolted along through the city to the outskirts, where
they stopped outside the prison gates. I was determined
not to show that I was afraid, and kept praying silently.
They ordered us to line up and remove our shoes, and
forced us to enter the prison barefoot, in disgrace. The
sharp sandy gravel cut our feet. It was clear that they
wanted to humiliate us right from the beginning. In
reception, we were taken one by one to be thoroughly
interrogated, and at last the guards came to take me to my
cell.

At least, I was expecting a cell. When they brought me
through the prison reception and out into the daylight in
the main compound, I was amazed. In front of me were
huge corrugated iron halls, similar to army barracks; this is
where the prisoners were kept. As we walked through one
of the halls I could see that there were hundreds of prisoners there, all emaciated and wearing shabby clothing.
Their suffering was etched on their faces. The hall they
took me to was divided into smaller rooms, with two sep-
arate rooms for solitary confinement and one room for
the guard on duty. Although prisoners were taken to a particular room, most were free to move around because the
doors were not locked.

I talked to some prisoners in one room who said that
they had been trying to escape to Italy, but had been caught
in Malta and sent back to Eritrea. Most of them were very

sick and could hardly walk. There was one man in particular who had heart problems and was suffering from diarrhoea. Because of this, he usually slept in the corridor.

I found this prison very hard, because so many people were sick. I found it impossible to sleep at night because I could hear people coughing and vomiting, and I felt I had to go to them and clean up. The man in the corridor needed to be helped to the toilet because he was too weak to stand alone, and for some of the time I was there, he was on an intravenous drip. There was only one doctor for the whole prison, and he was asleep most of the night, so often the sick man would beg me to stay with him. Consequently, I barely slept. So, although I was not physically beaten, the whole experience was torture for me.

There was another man who was an epileptic. He was often put in one of the tiny solitary confinement cells, but the outside wall of his cell was unfinished, so if he had a fit while he lay there he would knock stones out of the wall, which would land on him and bruise him. In the other solitary cell next to him was another man who would cry in pain all night, 'Please, I'm alone, will no one help me?' It was heart-rending. There were some Christians in my group, so we would pray for these men, but we were powerless to help them and we couldn't sleep through their distress.

We reported to the prison guards that the epileptic man kept injuring himself, and so they moved him into the corridor. We still couldn't sleep, but at least I could go and try to protect him when he had a fit. When they first brought him out he was bruised and bloody all over, so we washed him. He was a Muslim, and he couldn't understand why we wanted to help him. I told him about my faith and sang to him, and gradually he became curious and wanted to know more about Christianity. I had noticed that he always wore two charms on his belt. I pointed at them.

'Where did you get those charms from?'

'I saw a witch doctor, before I was arrested, about my fits. He said that they would make me better, but I should never take them off.'

'Jemal,' I said, 'those charms cannot heal you. Only prayer to God can do that.'

As I spoke he began to have a fit, and so I prayed for him. I did this often until, miraculously, he agreed to take the charms off. I took them away and burnt them, but whatever was in them smelled awful, and the guards demanded to know what I had been doing, which gave me the opportunity to explain to them that only prayer can heal a person, not charms from a witch doctor.

Jemal's health improved and his fits became less frequent. I was delighted, but he was worried.

'Helen, if they know that I am feeling better they will keep me here, and I want to be released.'

'If you continue to trust in God, no one can keep you from going home, not if God wills that you should be released.'

I was very pleased when he was released shortly afterwards.

One day, they brought a very smartly dressed man into our hall, and locked him in a room on his own. He looked like a businessman or a banker in his sharp tailored suit, and I wondered who he was. I walked past his cell late that night and he was shivering because they had not given him a blanket. I went straight to the guard's station and asked permission to give him my blanket. When I went in to give him the blanket he was very grateful.

'I was here on holiday,' he said. 'I work for the Saudi Arabian Embassy in Dubai, and today some men burst into my hotel room and brought me here. They won't tell me what I'm meant to have done.'

I felt sorry for him because he was treated very badly, so I tried to visit him as often as I could. He was handcuffed day and night, and suffered dreadfully from the fleas that everyone got in prison, especially since he couldn't scratch the bites. The guards often gave him tinned food, but would not remove the handcuffs so he could open the tins. Frequently he could not eat, unless I sneaked in to open them for him. This was very risky for me, as his door was often unlocked for just a short time. Because his was such a unique case, no one was supposed to know about him. They even took him to the toilet at night, while everyone was asleep.

The conditions in the prison were awful. It was infested with rats as well as fleas, and facilities were very basic. There were no toilets, just an open space behind the prison, so when I suffered from diarrhoea one night, a guard had to take me outside. It was after midnight, and clouds covered the moon. As we walked out I saw three shapes on the ground. At first they looked like sacks of potatoes or tied-up sheep, but as we passed them I saw that they were people. They were contorted; their wrists had been handcuffed behind them and then tied to their ankles. I thought they were dead until I heard one of them groan.

Shocked, I blurted out, 'What have they done? Will they have to stay there all night?' The guard just pointed at the waste ground and refused to answer any of my questions. Later, I asked the other prisoners about what I had seen and they told me that it is a common form of torture called the 'helicopter position'.

I had been at the military prison for three weeks when the guards came to my cell and told me to gather my belongings, because I was going to be moved. I assembled with a small group of Christians and they put us all into a military truck. I asked the woman next to me where we were going.

'I heard a guard say Mai Serwa.' She answered, her voice unsteady.

This was a notorious prison and military camp, reserved for dangerous, long-term prisoners and serious criminals.

5

Mai Serwa

Mai Serwa was in a deserted area outside the city. There was no fence around the prison – the land was so inhospitable that few prisoners tried to escape. I caught glimpses of it past the other prisoners as we jolted along a rough track; I thought there didn't seem to be much there. There were a few mud-brick huts that seemed to be military barracks and a larger mud-brick building that was the main prison office. Most of the buildings in Eritrea are stone-built, with proper bricks, so this seemed very primitive to me.

The guards hustled us off the truck and handed us over. We were herded into the main building and the Mai Serwa prison guards carried out a full body search. It was humiliating, but I was determined that they would not see me flinch. They were checking for weapons and money, but also Bibles. Of course, since we had just come from another prison, we had nothing.

They lined us up and marched us into the main compound. The whole place was dry and dusty, without a single tree or shrub. I thought the mud huts might hold toilets or showers, but I couldn't see any cells. We walked through the camp and down into the valley, where there were a lot of metal shipping containers – the kind that are used to transport goods overseas. These must be for storage, so where, I thought, are the cells? The site seemed large, so I assumed that they would lead us further in to wherever the cells were.

We were standing in line, waiting for the next order, when suddenly I caught a flash of movement. One of the containers nearest us had a small hole cut in the side, at around head height, and I could see people peeping out at us. Although I could only see part of their faces, it looked like there was a man and two younger boys. I felt the shock run through me. The containers *were* the cells.

I couldn't stop thinking about a recent news article. Some farmers had found an empty container and put their sheep in it overnight, thinking that it would be shelter for them. However, the temperature had dropped so much during the night that the container had become too cold and every sheep froze to death.

A guard gave the order to march forward, and I saw another struggling to wrench open the rusty double doors of another container. I forced myself to breathe deeply, to take in the warmth of the sun on my face and the feeling of space all around me, for I did not know when I might experience these things again. Abruptly the light dimmed as I followed the other women into the container. We turned in time to see the guard grin as he shoved the doors closed. They slammed together with a clang, leaving a thin strip of light, and then, as he leant against them and worked the bolts into place with a screeching noise that grated on my ears, the doors shut with a final-sounding pop, as the rubber seal trapped us inside. It felt as though the walls of the container had been forced inward as the air rushed out.

The only light filtered sluggishly in through a hole, no larger than a paperback book, hacked roughly into the side of the container at the far end. Panic-stricken, the woman beside me clutched at me. The container was no more than 20 feet long, so we were packed closely together. There were eighteen of us inside – the maximum a container can hold if everyone is to be able to lie down. Although I was not claustrophobic, it was hard to remain calm in such a small space so tightly packed with other frightened people.

I felt an itch on my leg and reached to scratch it, and then noticed everyone around me was doing the same. We quickly realized that the container was infested with fleas and lice and, as it must have been standing empty for a while, that they were very hungry.

I couldn't decide which was worse. Fleas can jump astonishing distances and are far too fast to catch. Lice are much slower, but to catch them you have to find them. They are very good at hiding in the hems of your clothes, but they are colourless so you can't see them, even in good light. Within minutes we were all scratching furiously, which actually makes the itching worse, as it breaks the skin. Very soon I felt as though my whole body was burning.

As the day wore on the container began to heat up, until it became almost too hot to bear. Many of the women began to complain of headaches. There were two teenage girls with us who were the worst affected by the heat and lack of air. Soon most of us had taken some of our clothing off in an attempt to keep cool.

The container was obviously old, with patches of rust and a pool of stagnant water in the corner. We were not allowed out to use the toilet; when one of the women had asked, a guard had shouldered past us into the container, grinning, with a large bucket.

Everyone was very despondent, and many of the women were angry. They asked me what we should do and I knew they were expecting me to say that we should shout or bang the container, to let our captors know that we were not going to tolerate this treatment. But I remembered a passage in Richard Wurmbrand's book, *Tortured for Christ*, about how Christians, like nightingales, could not be prevented from singing even in captivity, and I suggested that we sing: 'We should praise God in spite of the fleas, in spite of the lice, in spite of the heat. We should thank God despite our circumstances.' So I began to sing with them, and pray, and share the Word of God from memory.

When night came, the container grew very cold, very quickly. There was only just enough room for us to sleep side by side, and because the floor of the container alternated between wooden slats and the metal frame, it was never really level. In addition, it was tipped a little, so that all the condensation that dripped from the roof collected in a black and rusty pool in one corner. We had put the toilet bucket in the corner, but the smell became so bad that we had to sleep in shifts, to make sure that no one spent the whole night beside the bucket, or beside the pool of water. The best place to sleep was towards the middle, so we let the teenage girls and several of the older ladies have that spot. That first night, I was too cold to sleep much, and when I needed to use the bucket I had to crawl on hands and knees over the sleeping people, as it was too dark to see where to put my feet.

At 5 a.m. the container doors were opened at last, and the guards ordered us out. I was so thankful for the grey light of dawn, and fresh air. They made us carry the smelly bucket and marched us to an open space almost half a mile away, with no privacy. This, they told us, was the toilet field, and we were expected to use the toilet at this time every day. The bucket was for during the night, and every morning we had to take it with us and empty it.

As we lined up to go back into our container I could see more people, all male, spilling out of the container next to us, supervised by a guard. Looking around at all the containers that surrounded us, more than twenty, I calculated that if each held eighteen people, there were probably several hundred of us in the camp. There seemed to be a mixture of men and women, mostly aged between 20 and 30. I was appalled that so many young people were here, wasting their youth locked in containers. How could this possibly help our country to grow and flourish?

One of the guards saw me staring and rapped me on the back of my legs with his baton. 'Do not concern yourself with looking at the other prisoners,' he said. 'You have enough to think of with your own situation.' He slammed the doors behind us.

When he had locked us in and left, many of the women were furious and upset, and began to complain and cry. I tried to find ways to encourage them, and to make our situation more bearable. I encouraged everyone to sit on the floor in a circle and I began to speak to them.

'Remember that the walls of Jericho came down because of praises. If we keep complaining, we cannot win. Instead we must continue to pray, praise and sing. Satan wants to use discouraging words as a weapon against us, so we must continue to praise God in all circumstances.'

I could see some of the women nodding.

I continued, 'When the Israelites were approaching the Promised Land they sent spies ahead. Many of them returned saying that the people were so huge the Israelites could not hope to beat them, and so they cried all night. But crying and complaining cannot solve our problems. Let us be like Caleb and Joshua. The larger our enemies are, the more of a feast they will make for us! Just think about the woman who suffered from bleeding and who believed that if she only touched the hem of Jesus' robe she would be healed. In the crowd she was the one who had faith and it was rewarded. We should not be like these people endlessly fighting amongst themselves. We should just reach out to Jesus and have faith.'

This helped us to feel more accepting of our situation, and so we got into the habit of talking about the Bible, praying and singing in the container every day. The guards noticed this and started to spy on us to find out what we were talking about.

One morning while we were singing, we heard the bolts squeaking back. The doors were flung open and there were three angry guards standing outside.

'Who was singing?'

Some of the women were afraid and said that it was not them, and so the guards left them in the container. Those who admitted that they had been singing, including me, were pulled out. The guards made us take off our shoes and run around outside. The ground was sandy with many small sharp pebbles, and they cut our feet. Then they made us squat on our haunches and leap forward like frogs. It is a children's game that is played a lot in Eritrea, and it's very difficult to do, especially with bare feet on gravel. Some of the women were very good at it, but I had never played it as a child and I couldn't keep my balance. One guard kept shouting at me to 'Jump!' but I just kept falling over, so he beat me with his stick. Then he said, 'Since you cannot stand on your feet, you will lie down,' and he made me lie on my side and roll across the gravel.

After they had tortured us, they asked us one by one to agree never to sing again. They saw our refusal to give up our faith as disloyalty to our country, now that the government had declared it illegal.

I replied, 'I am a singer, and so I cannot give it up. I will sing quietly so as not to disturb the other containers, but I will not stop.' Roughly half of the other women refused, too. The guards let us back into the container for an hour at midday, but then they called us out again. They beat one of the women on her back with a police baton in front of us all to try to frighten us into obeying, and she ended up badly hurt. Gradually the women became afraid or worn down by the torture, and they agreed to stop singing and were let back in. Eventually there were just three of us left outside.

The guards ordered us to kneel on the gravel and brought three stones over, each heavier than the last. We each had to hold a stone above our head, so we had to do it in shifts, alternating between the lightest and the heaviest. One of the women was ill, and she kept vomiting whenever she tried to lift the stone. I took it from her and asked the guard to give her some water. But he just laughed at her.

'Are you sick because you're pregnant?' he kept asking.

It was a pointless exercise, designed to be painful and degrading.

We had to stay there until late at night, then they let us in. However, we began to sing again as soon as they had shut the door. They left us overnight, then at 10 a.m. they called five of us out again, including one of the young girls. They made us lie flat and tied our hands tightly behind our backs. It stopped our circulation and our hands went blue. I felt dizzy and thought I would faint. Then they untied us and asked if we would stop singing, and when we refused, they tied us up again. They repeated this throughout the day. When night came they left us tied outside in different places, so that we could not take comfort from each other, until 2 a.m., when they finally let us in. The three guards kept laughing at us. We couldn't believe how they treated us.

One of the women with me said, 'Don't they have wives or mothers themselves? I don't understand how they can treat women this way.'

Thankfully, when we prayed together we could forget our troubles for a little while, and draw strength from our faith.

I had been in prison for perhaps a month, when I wanted to listen to the radio one afternoon. I was curious about what was going on in the outside world. I knew that the people in the container opposite ours had a small radio, and so I looked out of the hole to try to catch their attention. Unfortunately one of the guards spotted me. He pulled me out of the container, tied me, and beat me. Then he forced me to sit, with my hands still tied behind my back, until late in the evening. It began to rain, so I was soon soaked and freezing cold. When he finally let me in my hands were swollen and I could hardly speak. The girls massaged me to get my circulation going, then kept me warm while I slept.

I still felt unwell the next morning when we went to the toilet, but when we came back the guard tied me again and left me outside, sprawled on the ground. The other prison guards shouted across to each other from the sentry towers, 'What happened to her? She was there yesterday!'

One of them joked: 'She looks like Jesus Christ on the cross.'

Later that day, the guard took me to an interrogator. I answered all his questions, but he still wasn't satisfied. He slid a paper across the desk between us.

'Why is this so hard for you to do, Helen? All I want is for you to stop singing. You should not follow this new faith, you should return to the religion of your father.'

'But I do follow my father's faith,' I replied. 'My parents are Bible-believers, and so am I. I do not follow any new religion. This is the same Bible that my grandfathers read in Geez (the church language of Ethiopia).

All that has changed is that it is now in the language of the people.'

He tapped a pen on the paper. 'Read this, Helen.'

It was a document saying that I would stop believing and would neither preach, praise, sing, nor spread the gospel. There was a space at the bottom for my signature. I looked at him steadily.

'I will not sign it.' I knew that by refusing I was condemning myself to prison for a long time, perhaps until I died, but I could not give up my God.

He persevered, saying, 'All you have to do is give up being a Christian, and we will let you go. Just say the word, and we will believe you.'

But I refused, and so he sent me back to the container to collect my belongings. I think he felt that I was a bad influence on the others in the container, and that I would find it much harder to defy him if he put me in worse conditions. So the guards moved me to a container which had just two other people in it – a lady who had been caught sneaking over the border into Sudan, and a woman who suffered from mental illness. This was to be the toughest period of my time in prison.

6

Melmesi

I spent ten months in the container with the mad woman. I learnt later that she had lived in America, but when she became mentally ill her friends sent her home to Eritrea, thinking that she would be better in the care of her family. She was the sister-in-law of a high-ranking general in the Eritrean army and had lived with him and his family until she tried to shoot him with his own gun. Because of his position in the army she was put in prison, but what she needed was proper psychiatric care. I never saw anyone give her any medication while she was in prison and, although she was still young, the stress of her situation had turned her hair completely grey.

Although I felt compassion for her, living with her was very hard. She would talk and cry without stopping, often all day and night, as she did not sleep very much. She would swear and insult the guards through the small window, and often she would fling herself against the walls to rock the container, or try to block the window with her blanket, cutting off our air supply. She was quiet to begin with, but gradually the guards started putting all the Christian women who had refused to abandon their faith into the container with us, and she became more unsettled. Eventually there were nineteen of us in a container which only had enough room for eighteen to lie down, and most nights we could not sleep. After she tried to strangle me, someone needed to stay awake to watch her, as she often attacked other people during the night when the candle had gone out and it was too dark to fight her off. Two girls from Eritrea's military college who had been caught praying had come to join us and they asked me if this was a prison or a psychiatric ward.

One morning we all got up for prayer, and a guard overheard me leading a Bible study. He handcuffed me outside the container throughout the hottest part of the day. At 4 p.m., one of the two prison chiefs came by.

'Ah, Helen. I see you are in trouble again. What have you done this time?'

I explained that we had all been unable to sleep because of the mad woman and so we had been comforting each other through prayer, as we were finding our situation very hard to bear. He scowled at me.

'You are spoiled, Helen! Do you think you are on holiday?'

'How can I be spoiled? You see the life I lead and the food I eat, and how I am beaten!'

He then began to question me about the mad woman. 'Do you think that she is really ill? She could be just pretending, in order to be released.'

I was horrified that he could even ask this. 'She is obviously a very sick lady. Sometimes she does not eat for three days, and she cannot sleep. Not even a very gifted actor could sustain this for so long.'

He just shrugged, and let me back into the container.

I became very thin over the months I spent imprisoned with the mad woman. I was not getting enough sleep and my body could not cope. The guards often teased me about how thin I was. My sister worked for the Ministry of Defence, and she asked the general to give her permission to see me. She brought my daughter Eva with her for a short visit, and I was delighted to see them both for the first time since I had been in prison. However, when they saw how ill I looked they both burst into tears.

'Will my mother die?' Eva sobbed, and I couldn't answer her, because so many people do die in Eritrean prisons.

Towards the end of that first year, the governor of all the prisons in Eritrea came to give an address to the prisoners. He inspected the containers, and then poked his head into our container. He had been told that I was a Christian, and he sniffed dismissively and called me *melmesi*, a label that the politicians give us. The nearest I can get to it in translation is something like 'lame duck', and it suggests that we are good for nothing, a burden and a drain on society. I was angry, and I demanded to speak to him. Although the guards ordered me to be silent, in the end they took me to the prison chiefs' office and I sat with a guard opposite this man.

'Why did you say Christians are good for nothing? I had my own business and even hired people to work for it, so I was helping society, not draining it. And if we are so useless, why do you train Christians at the military camps?'

He looked as though he couldn't quite believe that a prisoner was daring to speak to him this way, so he snapped, 'In our army, we don't have people like you.'

'Then how is it that I know many Christians who were injured or killed in the war? To say it is not true is an insult to those who gave their lives for our country. I know that in the army if you want a treasurer you will look for a Christian, because they are trustworthy. If we are lame ducks then why give us responsibility?'

I did not pause to hear his answer, but went on, 'If we are free to believe in anything, or not to believe, why attack me for exercising my right to choose? Would you rather that young people drink and start fights or would you prefer them to be moral and work for their country, because that is what believers do?'

He lost his temper and spat insults at me, then lit a cigarette and threw me out of the office. I knew that I was taking a risk to challenge him, but I wanted to defend my faith.

Most things in prison were risky, though. The guards did not like us to speak up, or ask questions. It was especially risky to look out of the container. The guards usually became angry if they saw us taking an interest in anything that was happening, but I was often curious about the outside world.

On one occasion a guard caught me peeping through the opening, pulled me outside and slapped and kicked me repeatedly. One of the medics was distributing tablets and was so shocked that he asked the guard to stop, pointing out that all I had done was to look outside. The guard was so incensed that the medic had questioned his authority that he dragged me round to the guards' quarters and beat me mercilessly with his fists all over my body. I did not say anything, just held his gaze as he punched me. He handcuffed me and left me until late evening, when one of our prison chiefs came past and asked what the problem was.

'I cannot tell you what the problem is,' I replied. 'Why don't you ask the man who beat me why he did this?'

The prison chief sent for the guard and afterwards the guard came to speak to me. He said, 'Why didn't you tell him what happened?'

I said, 'It is up to you to tell him what you did and why you did it. I will not tell tales about you. All I ask is that if you beat me again, you use a stick to beat me in an appropriate way. I am a woman and you should not have beaten me the way you did, with your bare hands.'

He let me go, but he had beaten me so severely that my period stopped for four months afterwards. The other prisoners urged me to tell one of the medics, but there was no point. I waited for the Lord to prompt me to speak up, but until he did I would not say anything. In prison everyone speaks the same language; all the prison staff are on the same side. If I had gone to the medic to report what the guard had done he would have told me to recant my faith and be released. He would treat my injuries but he would tell me that I was getting what I deserved, because I chose to be in prison by holding on to my faith.

In prison they did their best to take away our dignity, to make us less than human. Often they would over-salt the food so that it was inedible, and if anyone complained they would shrug and tell us to drink more water. The food in prison was usually tasteless mush. For a long time we were given lentil soup, which was really just hot water with lentils scattered in it. Often we would just be given bread and tea, so our teeth suffered because we were not getting enough nutrition. If one of us had diarrhoea, which happened a lot, and asked to be taken to the toilet field, the guards would usually refuse and make the person use the bucket.

One day, I put on my trainers to go to the toilet field, and all the guards thought that I was planning to escape. So they watched me use the toilet through binoculars, and I felt embarrassed when one of the guards told me about this when I came back. Another morning I was a little longer than usual and when I returned one of the guards stopped me and questioned me.

'Why are you late? There is nothing there to look at, and no flowers for you to pick.'

He was right; it was a clay field pitted with stones, and full of human waste. But even the prison chiefs had to use it, because there were no other facilities.

One morning there was a rumour that I had money and was going to distribute it, so the guards watched me closely again. They searched everywhere, even the plastic bag we used for litter. Eventually they watched me whenever I left the container to collect water or use the toilet, and I began to go to the toilet just once a day rather than twice. I started to turn pale, especially my eyes, because I did not get enough sunlight. The medic told me to go outside more and to exercise. So I started to exercise for an hour every day inside the container. The guards didn't like this because when I jogged on the spot it made a lot of noise, and often everyone else would join in.

Gradually people were moved around, so there were eventually only eight people in my container. The mad woman had also been moved, so we slept much better. It was the time of the European New Year (we have two New Year celebrations in Eritrea) and a lot of new prisoners arrived, enough to fill five containers with women and two with men. The guards warned us that when we went to the toilet we should not even look at these new people.

They re-interrogated every prisoner, and they finished with my container. I was the only Christian there, and they interrogated me so thoroughly that it was as if I was a new prisoner, too. It was always difficult for me when new prisoners came, because the guards made an example of me. They would torture me in front of the new people to scare them into behaving well. After my interrogation this time they moved me to a new container, which already held eighteen Christian women who had refused to give up their faith.

We were very overcrowded, but I was happy to join a Christian group again. Since I was the longest-serving prisoner, I took charge. I wanted to help them as much as I could, because I knew they would be comforted by the thought that someone cared for them. I would fold the older ladies' blankets when they went out to the toilet in the morning, and I would stay behind to clean the container. Many of them were worried about their husbands and children, so I tried to keep them busy and establish a routine. I would start by preparing breakfast; at this point we got four bread rolls each, two in the morning and two in the evening, with weak lentil soup, and a cup of tea. Then I would lead a Bible meditation and then I would sing. A month after I was first imprisoned I had managed to smuggle a Bible past the guards. I can't tell you exactly how I did it, as people still use this method and it is important that the authorities don't find out how it's done, but I can say that it was a whole Bible split into five smaller sections. This made it easier for me to hide it. Previously I had just read it alone, but now we did group readings every day. I also sang new songs to the group that I had written in prison.

It was an incredible experience to share my imprisonment with others who were also imprisoned for their faith. However, with Christians from six different denominations in one container, we often found that we disagreed. For example, there was one lady who was a traditional Orthodox Christian; a very strong believer. If I told a joke as part of my Bible teachings she disapproved, so she actually began to pray and worship alone, and even eat alone. I found it amazing that even in a container she would not socialize with Christians she perceived to be too worldly! Other people argued over how we prayed. Some people preferred to pray silently, while others would pray out loud, and in such a small space it was easy to see why this was a problem.

I had to remind them, 'We are not in our churches now. In our own church halls we can do as we please, but here we must tolerate each other's differences. If we keep fighting they may send us to the underground prisons in the mountains, so we must be thankful for our freedom to worship together here, and not argue about the ways we used to worship when we were free.'

The atmosphere inside the container was often worse than outside among the prison guards.

There were also differences in character which became difficult to cope with when we were shut up together for twenty-four hours at a time. Some of the ladies were very particular about where our few possessions were kept, and would nag the others, 'Why did you put that cup there? Put it over there instead!' Since I had been there the longest, other prisoners had left their clothes and possessions behind for me when they were released. At this stage, I had twelve blankets, and all the cups in the container belonged to me! I solved the problem by calling for one of the guards and asking him to leave each person one cup, one plate and one blanket, and to pack the rest up and give it to the prison chiefs to distribute to other prisoners. After this, things became more settled, and eventually we even managed to share communion together. I continued to teach from the Bible and to write teachings to other prisoners on paper that was smuggled in by some friends I had made among the guards.

One day, I was given a letter by one of the women in my container. She had come in with a man who had been a doctor, who was also arrested for his faith, and he had managed to pass her this letter. He wrote: 'Helen, everyone is being released but you have been here for a year. Why are you still in prison?'

Around this time I had begun to teach a little about Christianity to one of the other prisoners. He was a former soldier who was caught crossing to Sudan, and he was one of the most trusted prisoners in the compound. It was his job to distribute the bread rolls every morning to all the containers. Whenever he came to ours I would teach him about the Bible. I wrote a reply to the doctor and I dropped it into the bread basket. However, I did not realize that one of the guards up in the sentry box had seen me. He came down and stopped the soldier on his rounds, and read the letter.

Everyone was out at the toilet and I was tidying the container as usual, wearing a thin dress because it was so hot. The guard pulled me out and beat me until he broke his stick, then handcuffed me beside the soldier all day. I was in great pain because my dress was too thin to have protected me from his blows.

The guard called the man who had sent me the letter into the office for questioning. I felt guilty when I heard this, because I had put his real name rather than a code name when I wrote back to him. However, when he explained to the guards that he had just been asking me why I had not yet been released, they let him go. He felt guilty when he realized I had been punished, and he tried to persuade the guards that it was not my fault, but it was no use.

The guards left me handcuffed outside from 5 a.m. until 11 p.m. Then the guard who had caught me took me to an empty container. It was very old, rusty and full of holes. He pushed me inside, still in my thin dress, and fastened my hands in front of me. Then he locked the door. I lay there on the icy floor, without a blanket, and shivered. I struggled up, because I was afraid that if I lay down to sleep I would freeze to death like the sheep, but my whole body ached from the cold and the beating. I couldn't move about much, though, because it was too dark to see.

So I began to sing. I composed a song and repeated it all night.

> I love you, that's why I draw myself closer to you
> I know that it's worth following you.
> I am not only ready for prison, but I trust you until death.
> Even in a closed space or in a pit I will not surrender to evil spirits,
> Not even if I am bound or I am chained and I am suffering from cold,
> I will sing and I am not going to tire of singing, nor give up.
> My heart is burning with your love,
> And my heart declares I will never stop respecting you or lifting you up.
> I will sing again and again,
> I will sing a melody for you,
> My soul is pleased to sing for you.

At around six the next morning they pulled me out to interrogate me, but I was so cold I couldn't speak or walk. I tried to answer their questions but I couldn't make my lips form the words. So they left me handcuffed outside in the sun until I had warmed up, then they told me to read my letter aloud.

They had found the letter difficult to understand. I had written: 'The church is in a terrible situation, and there is no free worship. I cannot think about being released myself when every day the church is being destroyed.' This was from the book of Haggai, and I knew that the Christian doctor would understand it, but the guards did not. I also quoted from Nehemiah, when the walls of Jerusalem were broken down and he prayed and fasted, and about Shadrach, Meshach and Abednego, writing: 'This time the gold statue is replaced by a piece of paper.' So the guards had punished me, even though they hadn't understood what I had written.

'Why,' one of the guards asked, 'are you just writing what is written in your Bible? Why don't you use a common language, rather than these complicated words?' He ordered me to stop writing letters to other prisoners.

I said, 'I was arrested because I preached and spread the gospel, and even now I will not stop. I will continue to write and speak about my faith.'

So they put me in solitary confinement.

7

Solitary

For the first few days I was on my own in a container, and then they put another woman in with me. She was bruised all over, and often cried out in pain, and could not sleep during that first night. There was a strange smell about her, as though she had a wound that had become infected. She told me that she had been beaten with police batons, and I asked her to let me look at her injuries. I discovered that there were lumps all over her body, and the smell was a prolapsed uterus. They had beaten her so badly that her uterus was actually hanging outside her body. Her ligaments were damaged and it would not stay inside, so we had to keep pushing it back into place. I tried to massage her limbs to help her circulation and bring the swellings down, but since she had not had any medical care when she was first tortured, it seemed to be too late to help her. She should have been in hospital, but after a few days they transferred her to another container and I was alone again.

Although I was lonely at first, I actually came to enjoy my time in solitary confinement. It was fruitful because I managed to write words of encouragement and Bible teaching to other prisoners. I wrote under a blanket so that if the guards looked in they would not see me, and often I would write up to sixteen pages of letters to fellow prisoners. I even had a radio that I had managed to conceal amongst my belongings when they transferred me to solitary confinement, so I could follow the news and listen to some spiritual programmes.

I also had three cats that had belonged to one of the other prisoners. When his cat had two kittens he released them and they began to wander between containers. They spent so much time with me that everyone began to call them 'Helen's cats'. They would wait until I went to the toilet in the morning and then sneak in when the door was opened, or sometimes they would try to jump from the roof through the small opening. I fed them on small pieces of my own rations every morning and they would spend the whole day with me. I loved to watch them playing. They were also very useful when I wanted to send my letters to other prisoners. I would tie a length of thread around each of their necks, and fold a scrap of paper around it under their chin. Because the thread was so thin, it could not be easily seen against their fur. I would then let them out and they would sneak round the other containers in search of food. The other prisoners knew to check the cats' necks for my letters.

I also wrote a lot of songs, but unfortunately the guards came to search the container and took them all away. Many people suffered mental breakdowns as a result of being in solitary confinement, so the guards thought that this would be the harshest punishment yet, and would break my spirit. In fact, I really enjoyed my time alone.

During this time, one of the prison guards had taken a rare holiday, and he was late in returning, so they locked him in a container for three days alone as punishment. When they released him, he came to my container and spoke to me through the opening.

'Helen, I have just had three days in a container and I couldn't bear it. How is it that after all this time you are still all right?'

He could not believe that I could be calm there, let alone content.

Many people become depressed when they are kept for any length of time in solitary but I found it to be one of the most enjoyable times I spent in prison. I actually wished that I could have more time because I did not have a chance to write everything that came to me in the silence.

I had a routine: I would wake and pray, read and study my Bible, then write songs and write to prisoners, then exercise. So it seemed to me that every day was full. I was still curious to see other people, though. One day, I put my face to the opening and a guard was right outside.

'What are you doing?' he snapped.

I replied, 'I am just looking to see what is happening outside.'

He handcuffed me outside my container, but all the other prisoners started to complain from inside their containers.

'She is on her own. You cannot possibly find any excuse to punish her!' I heard them shouting. 'She has done no harm to anyone. It is natural when alone to be curious and to want to see the outside world.'

I told him, 'What you are doing is totally unacceptable. You should not be punishing me for looking outside, when you are supposed to let me out to get fresh air every day.' The guard was embarrassed, especially when the other prisoners agreed with me.

Although I was alone, I was often aware of God's presence. One of the prison guards developed an obsession with me and kept coming to my container to see me.

One day, he called to me through the window: 'I cannot live without you. Will you marry me?'

I was taken aback, but I explained gently, 'I am in prison. How can I possibly think of getting married?'

However, he was persistent and was always watching me when I left the container. I became very uneasy, and when he kept asking me to be his wife I became really frightened. Many of the guards treated female prisoners like slaves, demanding sex and often raping them. I knew there was a real possibility that one day he would follow me to the toilet field and then rape me. I could end up pregnant, or infected with HIV. He would receive a very light punishment, if he was punished at all, but for me it would be a life sentence.

One day, I felt so afraid that I knelt weeping in my container and prayed, 'Please, God, help me. Please make him leave me alone.' The next day the guard was dead.

A guard had been transferred from another prison, and they had quarrelled, and the new guard had shot him. The murderer was given fifteen years and imprisoned in the container next to mine. I was horrified, and for a long time I was racked with guilt that it was my fault this man was dead because I had asked God to release me from him.

However, I also saw God turn an evil plan to good. In prison the guards often select people as spies, to keep an eye on troublesome prisoners. One day, they brought two girls to my container. Their names were Rahel and Elsa. They were both in the army before they were arrested. They were supposed to spy on me and report back, because the authorities could not understand how, despite their treatment of me, I was still defiant. However, things backfired because the girls really liked me. Very soon we had become good friends and they even told me, 'We were supposed to spy on you. But we like you, and so we won't!'

We came to love each other like sisters. Once, we were sharing a gabi shawl, which we had spread over all three of us, and a guard came by. He said, 'You cannot share that, you should each use your own. Did Helen make you do this?'

But the girls laughed, and said, 'No. We cannot follow Helen's example. We are not fortunate enough to be like her. She is unique.'

Since the girls were not spying as they had been told to, Rahel was released, but they left Elsa in the container with me for a while. Rahel left all her spare clothes for me. This was a blessing as for a long time I had not been allowed any more clothes, even when the old ones wore out. I felt that this was God's provision for me, like the ravens he sent to Elijah. It was my experience that no matter what hardship I was in, God always sent someone to help me. So, although these girls were sent to spy on me, God used them to bless me.

One early morning I was listening to a Christian programme on my little radio when the guards opened the container without warning and confiscated the radio. By this stage they were using every opportunity to put pressure on me to get me to sign the paper to recant my faith. They knew that I followed the news and that the radio brought pleasure to my life and they wanted to hurt me by denying me that joy. I found it very hard in the days after they took the radio but eventually accepted that I must manage without it.

However, there was a group of long-term prisoners at Mai Serwa who had been officers in the army, and they were given newspapers and books, so they began to pass the newspapers on to me. They gave me so many that the papers started to pile up in my container. I was delighted to have news of the world outside the prison. I read a special series on people who had changed the world, such as Rosa Parks who stood up against segregation on buses, and I began to fasten these articles around the walls of my container, using chewing gum to stick them in place. I found their stories very inspiring and I would often meditate on them.

One day, a guard came to my container and, looking in, he asked me about them. When I had explained, he said, 'Don't you realize you are one of these people?'

I had enjoyed my solitary confinement for four months when one of the interrogators came to my container and ordered me to gather together my belongings. I was going to be moved to a container with seven other ladies, on the strict understanding that I would not teach, preach or sing. I told him that I could not comply with that and asked him to leave me in solitary, but he had already begun to collect my things.

8

Less Than Human

Two of the ladies in my new container were believers. I already knew one, whose name was Ester, but the other girl was new. Her name was Liya. I was delighted to discover that they had their own radio. We established a routine of listening to spiritual programmes and then praying and studying the Bible. Then I began to sing for them, and it wasn't long before there was a rattling at the door and a guard shouting, 'Who is singing?'

Liya claimed that it was her, and so he took her outside and chained her for the whole evening.

When he came to let us out the next morning, the guard said, 'She was not singing alone. You two were also singing.' He chained us both outside with Liya from early morning until 2 a.m., and again the next day.

When two days had passed, he sent everyone else to the field for their toilet break, but warned us never to sing again. Of course, we refused. He then pulled me aside: 'If I hear you sing once more, I will take you to sleep with the male prisoners.' This was the worst threat a guard had made so far. He pushed me back into the container, which stood open while everyone was at the field, but left Liya outside. Since she was new and had been protecting me I felt very sorry for her, so I slipped out again and went to sit with her.

When the guard saw me, he said, 'What do you think you are, Helen, a priest comforting your people? I told you to get back in the container.'

But I refused. 'Please let me stay with her, or chain me on her behalf.'

The guard could not understand why I would do this, so he called for three higher-ranking guards to come to speak to me. I explained that I would like to either be punished in her place, or to be allowed to stay and comfort her. The senior guards weren't sure what to make of this either.

The first guard shook his head.

'If you are this serious with your faith, Helen, you must be prepared for the harshest punishment. You would be wiser to give up your beliefs before it is too late.'

Liya was grateful to me for my support, and we became good friends. I learnt that her father and mother had both been bush fighters who had fought for Eritrea's independence, and that she had been born in the bush. She was so bold, and I was impressed by her faith. Even non-believers were stunned by her love and service. For example, every day she would clean out the container and take the toilet bucket out, not only without complaint, but happily. Even when I asked her to let me take a turn, she refused, telling me that she saw it as her job – a way in which she could serve God and serve others every day. She also loved to write Bible teachings, so I joined in and Ester illustrated them; she had been an engineer before she came to prison. The three of us made a good team, and we would send our illustrated Bible teachings round to other prisoners.

While I was in the container with Ester and Liya the guards told us that they had run out of lentils, so we would have to survive on military rations. These were dry biscuits or crackers, given out twice a day with a cup of tea. We had been surviving on these for around a month when one of the prison officers called me to his office. I had not seen my daughter for many months, and I was convinced that he had called me because she was here to see me. But when I got to his office, it was empty. He made me sit down opposite him, and then he shook his head.

'Helen, don't try to pretend you don't know what I'm talking about. You were seen accepting a bag of *tihni* from one of the guards.' Tihni is a high-calorie cereal food, a bit like porridge oats, that we usually mix with water. It is very useful for long journeys, and especially for prisoners who are starving, as we were.

I was furious. '*Tihni*!' I shouted. 'This is nonsense!'

I was too upset to speak to him, both because of the false accusation and because I was bitterly disappointed not to see Eva. I asked to go back to my container, but he refused. I told him firmly, 'No one has given me anything, so whoever told you this must be mistaken. If you did have a guard who was handing out food, though, you should be proud of him for his compassion. Yes, we are prisoners, but we still have human needs. Yet you never cared about any of that, and now you dare to accuse me of this. It is not a crime to need food, but even when we are sick you do not feed us properly. You give us salt and sugar when we have diarrhoea, but no medicines or nutritious food.'

I think he was embarrassed, because he didn't reply, just motioned for me to return to my container.

Another prison governor came to visit. Often when official visits took place, the senior guards would ask for two volunteers to come and speak to the governor. However, since we were punished if we complained about the conditions in prison, when they came round to our container everyone kept quiet.

So the prison governor said, 'Helen, this question is for you. Why are all Christians anti-government?'

I could not keep silent. 'We are not anti-government. In fact, we support the government and are good for the authorities and for the country. When I had my own business I always paid my taxes and did all that was asked of me. All Christians are willing to participate in military service. I could not go before because of my daughter, but if you want me to go now, I will go.' Then I quoted from the Eritrean Constitution: 'Doesn't the constitution say, "The country is for all of us but religion is a private matter"? Yet you do not allow us to practise our faith, so you are against the constitution. We will not abandon our faith, but we would do anything for our country.'

This made him angry. Very few prisoners argue with the officials in this way, with clear and coherent arguments. Sadly, he was too angry to listen to me any more, and the guards transferred the believers in our container to another one, as punishment. This new one was right at the edge of the group and it was in the full sun – the outer containers shade the inner ones and are only used for troublesome prisoners. Our new container was so hot it was unbearable, so we complained.

The prison guards just shrugged and said, 'You have the right to choose. Either choose to sign the paper to say you will not practise your faith, or choose to stay in the sun.'

Since they had originally produced the paper for me to sign, they had asked me – and the other Christian prisoners – to sign several more times, usually when new prisoners arrived.

They made us stay in the container in the heat, but they called Liya out. Her father was working hard to get her released. He had recently visited and told her to abandon her faith, but she had refused. He had come again for a meeting with the prison guards.

I was sitting in the container with Ester when the door opened and Liya came in holding what looked like a ball of black cloth in both hands. Then we realized it was some of her hair. At the meeting her father had tried to convince her again, and she had refused. He became so angry that he grabbed her by the hair, and most of it came out in his hand, leaving her with a bald patch. He beat her so badly that the guards were forced to intervene. We helped her cut what was left of her hair off. Shortly afterwards the guards moved her to a solitary container because they said I was brainwashing her, but she just laughed and told them that they were wrong.

One day, Liya's mother came to visit and brought her a bag of bananas and some money. Liya wanted to give some of the money to me because she knew I had none in prison, but the guards were constantly watching us. So when we went to the toilet field she tucked some money under the bananas and gave me the whole bag. I had enough time to take the money out before the guards spotted us and made me give the bananas back to her. We still managed to send letters between the containers though, and when they put some ladies who had been caught crossing the border in Liya's container, she converted them. The guards could not stop her preaching either. Eventually she was transferred to another prison, and I heard that she was finally released.

One day, someone in a neighbouring container saw me glance out of the window and said, 'Hi.' The guard saw and asked the man who he was talking to. I was very sick with diarrhoea, but they pulled both of us out of our containers and handcuffed me. Then they put a stick under his knees and tied his feet and hands, then turned him upside down, and left us like that all day in the sun. He was in prison for a long time and I heard that he died shortly after he was released.

As I wrote to so many of the prisoners, I came to know their stories too. One lady developed a phobia of the sound the doors made as they sealed and the air rushed out. She wrote to me to ask how I had survived for so long in prison. Later she had a nervous breakdown and was taken to a psychiatric hospital. This was a common problem in prison. One man who was caught trafficking people out across the border also had a nervous breakdown. He never had any visitors because his family lived by the border with

Sudan and couldn't travel, so he must have felt that he had been abandoned. Another elderly man was a Jehovah's Witness, which was one of the banned religions, and he was brought to prison at the time when they had stopped families bringing food in for Christians and Jehovah's Witnesses. After a few days he began to scream that he was hungry, and when the guards opened his container he threw stones at them; he too suffered a breakdown.

Those people who had been kept in the containers for a long time would often experience sharp pains in their legs and the medics usually suggested a few minutes in the sunshine. I saw one man ask the guard for this, because he had a letter from the medic to say that he needed it. The guard pulled him outside then began to whip him as we all watched.

Another form of torture was to chain or handcuff people in their container. One prisoner was chained night and day, and when they let him out for the toilet or to fetch water, the guards would only take the chain off one leg. Then they would try to get him to move faster, but the chain was too heavy. One of the guards started to beat him outside my container and I screamed for him to stop.

All prisoners suffer when they see someone else suffering. Even those prisoners who are not beaten much may develop illnesses in prison such as diabetes or depression, so when they are finally released their suffering continues.

The authorities caught a young man trying to cross into Sudan. He was tall and strong, and when he was brought to the container he asked politely to speak to the chief of the prison. But the guard refused, and when the young man asked again, the guard pushed him over, then grabbed him by the neck and banged his head repeatedly on the ground. We all shouted for him to stop, but when the young man recovered he was very depressed and lost weight, because of this humiliating treatment.

Most of the guards delighted in finding degrading and demoralizing punishments for us. One of their favourites was to take us to the toilet field and order us to bring a rock back. Then the next day we would have to carry it back to the field. One of the new prisoners was a teacher and he refused, saying that they should use punishments that were more appropriate. Of course, he was beaten.

It is astonishing how many people in Eritrea have been in prison, and often they do not know why. Some prisoners were collected from their houses while they were sleeping at night. Most were well-educated people and were never given a reason for their arrest. Usually they would be held for six or seven months, often without interrogation and almost always without trial or conviction. Then they would be released and told not to do it again! This is very common; it is a form of psychological torture. It is likely that the reasoning behind it, especially when the prisoners are educated people, is 'Perhaps they're plotting against the government, or at least they disagree with some of the government's actions' so the authorities try to frighten them in case they had been thinking of rebelling. In the vast majority of cases, these people are law-abiding citizens and the government's treatment of them is totally unfounded.

This is exactly what had happened to a family who came to our container. The mother and daughter stayed with us, while the father was in the men's section. They were all arrested in the middle of the night and taken to prison with no explanation. The daughter was only 17, and within minutes of getting into the container her whole body started to swell up. She must have been allergic to one of the parasites in the container, because they had to take her to hospital.

Punishment is usually harshest for Christians in prison. I tried to comfort a Christian man who was caught trying to leave the country. They beat him with a stick until they damaged his spine. He had two sticks to help him walk but he had to drag his legs along behind, and he was worried that he would no longer be able to work. In Eritrea the handicapped are usually seen as dead weight, worse than useless. It is very important to Eritreans to be able to benefit our country, so to be crippled is a terrible thing.

Some time later, another group of Christians were transferred to our prison. They had been in prison for four years. They were not allowed to receive food from their families and were forced by the guards to work as part of their punishment – moving stones and carrying 20-litre buckets of water between containers. It was pointless and degrading.

One day, the prison guards were having a small party and they were roasting corn on the cob. The smell was delicious. I said to one of them, 'It's been a long time since we tasted anything that smells so good. Why don't you give us some?'

But he shouted, 'You were not created to eat food like this. You should not even be allowed to smell it!'

To some guards, Christians were less than human. Sometimes they would forget to give us water or take us for a shower or to wash our clothes. Once a guard took us to the tap, but there was no bowl. When we asked him for a bowl, he told us that we would have to do without it. We were forced to wash our clothes on the stony ground.

However, in a strange way, the terrible situation Christians were in made other prisoners feel better. New prisoners usually complained about the conditions until they saw how the Christians were treated. One day, a new prisoner came to me and asked me how long I had been there. I had been there more than two years but I told him it was less than two, as I didn't want to discourage him. He was amazed, and asked me if it was for murder!

Although the guards often treated us badly, I sometimes felt sorry for them. After all, they too spent their lives in prison. They were there when I was arrested, and many are probably still there now. Because they were there as part of their military service, they were not paid a wage but were just given their food and accommodation, and they would work every day of the week, with perhaps two weeks off in six months. Their faces were always sad. They also did not manage to sleep properly, because they worked in shifts. Often a guard would have only two hours' sleep before being woken for his next shift. The majority of the guards were not married because they could not go anywhere to meet people, and had no time to care for a family, so it is little wonder that so many of them were angry and bitter. They were often bored, and I once saw one guard ask another to do a crossword with him, telling him it would keep him awake.

The other guard replied, 'I have plenty of things to keep me awake here. Don't you have something that will help me sleep?'

The guards often said to us, 'Even we are not happy to be here.' Perhaps that is why they beat the prisoners so much.

Still, not all guards were the same. Some were kind, and would try to help, or to talk or listen to us. Some guards wouldn't call the medic even for prisoners who were very sick, while others would try to comfort them. Even in prison there are all types of people.

One day, they called me, Ester, and the other believers to the office. One of the prison chiefs was there and he presented us with a piece of paper that said, 'I will keep on preaching and believing.' It was a positive confession, the opposite of the last paper they had asked us to sign.

The prison chief said, 'This is your last chance. If you sign this paper, you will have to stay in prison and we will send you to one of the secret prisons, and you will never be released. If you do not sign it, then we will let you go. If you choose to sign, I wash my hands of you; you will have decided your own fate. What happens to you then will not be my fault.'

I reflected that every time they called us to the office it seemed as though things got worse. They always had an evil scheme in mind. Whenever I listened to the news and heard that Eritrea was in the top ten countries for human rights abuses, I always thought that it should be number one. Around 10 per cent of Christians in Eritrea are in prison at any one time, but in fact more than 50 per cent of us have been in prison at some time in our lives. It is worse, I think, than the death penalty. It would be kinder to kill us. Prison is a living death, and more than that, it is a death of dignity, hopes and dreams. Our situation reminded me of a Muslim man that I met in prison who was beaten severely about the head, and suffered long-term damage. He was not living, just existing, just as we all were in prison.

During the time when Eritrea was ruled by the Ethiopian dictator Mengistu, before we gained our independence, my father was arrested for supporting the previous government. He was held for more than a year but he was only tortured for the first few weeks while they interrogated him in a proper prison with modern facilities. After those first weeks we were allowed to see him. But now, the longer you are in prison the more they torture you, and the less they allow you to see your family. In all this time I had only seen Eva once.

But I still refused to give in to them. I told the chief, 'I cannot abandon my faith. If you puncture a sack of grain, the only thing that pours out is the type of grain that was in the sack. It is the same with me. I can only say what is inside me; everything that is in my heart must come out of my mouth. So give me the paper, and I will sign it, and then you can send me wherever you want.'

He told me to wait, to think about the consequences of making this decision. I felt this was cruel, as really for me there was no choice at all.

I told him, 'The more you punish me, the stronger I will be. If you keep hammering on a nail's head it just becomes harder to pull out of the wall. Give me the paper.' So I signed, and went back to my container.

I could not understand how they expected me to stop believing; it was impossible for me. In fact, the guards were making their own situation worse, because people began to ask what was so special about this religion that Christians refused to give it up, and they also began to believe. Our suffering became a glory for our faith.

On reflection, I think the authorities should understand by now that what they are doing doesn't work. I am convinced that the number of Christians has doubled or tripled since they closed the churches. So perhaps God is using this terrible situation for his glory.

9

The Sacrificial Lamb

Not long after that, another provincial governor came to visit the prison. One of the prison chiefs opened our container and the governor asked, 'Who are these ladies?'

The chief replied, 'They are the ones disturbing the whole society – followers of the Pentecostal religion.' Then he banged the door shut because he didn't want to give us a chance to try to convince the governor otherwise.

The other prison chief came and tried to convince us that we had been wrong to sign the paper, but I told him, 'Why come bothering us now? It is done.'

Yet another official visited and accused me of being anti-government. 'Political agents are using you,' he said. 'Why do you let them do this? Why do you risk your life to please other people and support their cause? Why make yourself a sacrificial lamb? Perhaps you are a genuine believer, but the ones who have asked you to stick so rigidly to this rebellious religion are just taking advantage of you for their political agenda.'

I said, 'If I may speak for myself: I have no other agenda but believing in the Bible. Since my childhood I have never had any other intention. This Bible is not new – my fathers and forefathers read it. I am reading the same Bible my grandfather read; the only difference is that he read it in *Geez* while I can read it in my language. He used to treat his Bible with special reverence and keep it in a sacred box, but I do not worry about handling mine. My grandfather went to church for fifty years but he didn't understand the Bible; we know it better because it is in our language. If you are trying to take us back to the days of the older generation, then you cannot care about what is best for our country. Everything is changing and we have to adapt and move with the times. Each generation of inventors must bring new ideas, otherwise we will have nothing new and nothing will change or improve. In our generation, because we can understand the Bible, people are changing.'

'I hate the Bible,' he growled, 'because it makes our people weak.'

I knew the guards had no respect for the Bible because they burnt them whenever they caught a prisoner with one. Even when people undertake their military service the authorities search them and burn any Bibles they find, so Eritreans really are not free to worship anywhere. They often call Christians 'Pentes', from 'Pentecostals'. It is a derogatory term for anyone who is serious about their faith. Christians in Eritrea do not swear, even though there is a culture of bad language, and when we don't they call us 'useless Pentes'.

Not long after this conversation, I prepared a Bible teaching for one of the prison guards. I had it ready for him around midday when it was quiet in prison and he could come and collect it. By chance, one of the senior guards saw him and asked him what the paper was, and he had to hand it over.

Since I had been teaching him for a while, I had written on the top of the paper 'Continuing from last lesson', so they knew that we were both serious about the lessons. They called me out of my container and handcuffed me next to my pupil, along with the guard who had been on duty. They fastened my ankles together as well, but they made the cuffs too tight so the pain was excruciating. They left us there the whole night and I was in too much pain to sleep. There was one word from the Bible that I continually read, and it came into my mind now. It was from Isaiah 53:2: 'He had no beauty.' I lay there, my legs throbbing, and I watched the stars come out. It seemed that I was very small beneath the vast expanse of the sky, and as though, at this reminder of God's majesty, the power the guards had over me was no longer so great. I concentrated on the stars, because if I let myself think of my legs the pain became unbearable. I was afraid that if the circulation was cut off for too long, I might lose them, and never be able to walk again, or work.

During the night most of the guards passed by as they changed shifts, and many of them laughed at us. A group of them stood and watched us, and I heard one say, 'Look at Helen! She looks like a sheep prepared for the holiday slaughter.'

The guard beside him shook his head. 'I would not want to eat that sheep. She is so dirty, she could be a beggar.'

When morning came I was almost delirious with pain, but I remember the other prisoners passing by on their way to the toilet, and many of them looked sympathetic. I saw my friend Ester, and as she looked at me, tears began to run down her cheeks.

They called us for interrogation, and I was so stiff I could barely walk. They brought us to the chief's office, and he interviewed us with an interrogator. They first questioned the guard who I had been teaching, asking him what I had been saying. He replied honestly, explaining in detail about the gospel, about Jesus and salvation. Then they produced a paper for him to sign, to say that he would stop believing. He signed it, because he was a new believer, and also because he knew that they would torture him if he did not. However, once he had signed they did not release him, and he ended up staying in prison for many months afterwards.

Then they turned to the guard who had been on duty, and demanded to know why he had not stopped us. He said that he had not seen anything, and they must have believed him because they released him after only four days. Then it was my turn. They asked me why I had been teaching members of staff.

'I am always looking for opportunities to talk about my faith,' I replied, 'and to spread the news about Jesus. I am not ashamed of the gospel, and I will talk to anyone and to everyone. Jesus does not just want me to tell the prisoners about him, he wants me to tell the guards too. Even if the president were to visit the prison, I would tell him about the gospel.' They looked furious, so I continued, 'I am not afraid of you. You can do what you want to me, but ultimately all you can do is kill my body, you cannot touch my soul. You cannot even kill me unless it is God's will that I should die.'

They had no answer for that, so they just returned me to my container.

However, that was not the end of the matter. There was another man in prison who had been caught trying to cross the border. As punishment, the guards had put him in the container opposite mine, which was reserved for those suffering with diarrhoea. Conditions were very unpleasant in that container, and he was desperate to reduce his sentence. So the prison guards recruited him as a spy, and his first task was to trap me.

He came to me and asked me to write him some Bible teaching. I agreed, but as I was already writing for a lot of other prisoners, it took me a while. He came and asked me again, and I felt sorry for him, so I copied out one of the teachings that Liya and I had written, then Ester illustrated it for me. I folded it up and hid it in a matchbox.

He came to stand outside the container, and I whispered, 'Is it safe?' He said it was, but he lied – the guard was watching. I threw the matchbox to him, and he caught it, and took it straight to the guard.

The guard came down with it to our container and said, 'Who threw this?'

I opened my mouth but Ester said, 'I did.'

Because I had been tortured so much, she did not want me to get into trouble again. When the guard saw the writing on the paper inside, though, he knew it was me.

He pulled us both out of our container. Ester wore glasses, and the guard took these off before slapping her face hard. He made her lie face down so that he could handcuff her, kicking her and leaving her moaning in pain. Usually when we were left fastened outside, they would allow us to sit. The punishment of lying face down was particularly cruel for women, because we found it hard to lie on our chests on the stony ground.

'Now,' the guard said, gleefully, 'we have evidence against you.'

He also handcuffed the spy, so that the other prisoners would not suspect anything, but he was soon released.

He came over to me. 'What are we going to do with you?' He stared fixedly at me. 'You are always making trouble.'

I instinctively put my hands up to my face, because I was sure he was going to slap me, too. Sure enough, he kept aiming blows at my face and I kept trying to dodge. It must have looked from a distance like we were boxing, as he jabbed and I bobbed and weaved. I was afraid that he meant to beat me until my face was disfigured.

My legs began to give way, and I slowly slid down to the ground.

'Where are all your writings, Helen?'

I realized that he thought I was copying out my teachings from books I had smuggled in.

I pointed to my head. 'They are all in there.'

He drew his boot back. 'Then they will be easy to erase.'

I felt as though something had exploded against the side of my head, as he kicked me repeatedly. I felt blows raining down on my body.

We were in the centre of the prison compound, and although it was evening and the containers were locked for the night, the other prisoners were watching and I heard them screaming for him to stop his brutal beating. Finally, he grew tired and kicked me hard in the ribs. 'Get up.'

He shoved me in the direction of my container, but I was dazed and it took me a long time to control my spinning head and wobbling steps. When I got there I collapsed, but I was unable to sleep because of the pain all over my body and a pounding headache.

The next morning I managed to limp out for the toilet break, but no sooner had we returned to the container than the guard called us again. I was so badly bruised from the beating that I had thought I wouldn't be called again for a while. They handcuffed both Ester and I outside, and then another guard came to say that one of the prison chiefs wanted to see me.

He led me through the narrow lanes between containers to the main part of the compound and the office. I have mentioned before that the prison actually had two chiefs; one was a man from an Orthodox family like me, and the other was the man now sitting at the desk in front of me – a Muslim called Suleiman. He had a large stack of my writings in his hands and he slapped them down on the desk with a bang, next to a police baton. I couldn't take my eyes off the baton. I remembered that another prisoner, who had been accused of stealing, had told me she had been beaten badly by Suleiman. A long-term Christian prisoner had also been beaten by him a month ago, and had written to tell me about it. Suleiman was systematic. He had started from the man's neck and moved around both arms, across his shoulders, down his back and all the way down both legs. Now I knew that the same thing was going to happen to me and, despite my faith, I was afraid.

When he began to speak to me I tried my best to calm him down, because he was so angry. I kept saying, 'Suleiman, it is not like this,' but it was as though he did not even hear me. He was determined to take out his fury on me.

Just before the first blow from his baton landed, a word from Isaiah 53:7 came to me: 'When he was beaten he was silent.' I fixed my mind on this, and drew strength from it. If Jesus had not cried out, I would not either.

Suleiman carried on beating me. It was supposed to be me who was screaming, but I remained silent. Instead, as each blow connected, he yelled, 'Leave us alone, Helen!' He had not bothered to chain me, because all the guards knew that the Christian prisoners did not fight back. As he continued and I still did not open my mouth, he obviously thought that he was not beating me hard enough, so he redoubled his efforts. Eventually he became tired from his exertions and said, 'We shall have a break, so that you can think about your actions.' All my muscles began to twitch involuntarily as I lay on the floor. He leant against his desk, placing the baton beside him, and gazed down at me.

'Helen,' he said, 'you must stop believing.'

How could he still think I would stop, after all that had happened to me? Did he really think that a beating would make me abandon my faith?

'Suleiman, you can do whatever you like to me, but I will believe and be faithful to my God, even if you kill me.'

He took a piece of paper from his desk and waved it at me. 'Then you must sign to say that you will not teach my staff members. You are teaching everyone, your writings are everywhere!'

I looked up at him from where I lay. 'Suleiman, I will not sign. There is only one thought in my head and that is to preach salvation to my brothers and sisters, wherever I may be.'

He snatched up his baton and began to beat every inch of me, from my head to my feet. I have never felt pain like it. Each blow seemed to leave behind a burning sensation, and soon I felt as though my body was on fire. Yet I clung to the words from Isaiah, and eventually Suleiman sat down and stared at me in amazement. I think he could not believe that I had not once cried out or begged him to stop.

He said, 'Well? Do you have anything to say?'

'No, nothing,' I replied. 'You are doing your job, and I am doing mine.'

He was confused. 'What do you mean?'

'You are fulfilling your purpose by beating me,' I explained, 'and I too am fulfilling mine.'

I meant that I was suffering for God. But in Suleiman's experience, everyone collapsed after such a beating, and his victims were often incapacitated for days. He ordered me to stand, and I struggled to obey. He called a guard and ordered him to take me back and chain me outside my container, because I hadn't changed my mind. As I left, he shook his head in astonishment.

The guard chained me next to Ester, with my hands behind my back. My hands were severely swollen because Suleiman had paid special attention to them as punishment for writing all my teachings. I felt that I could not bear the pain as they were handcuffed. I felt even worse when the guard took Ester to see Suleiman, because I was afraid he would do the same to her. I did not want her to suffer too; also, if we were both badly beaten, there would be no one to care for us because, at that time, we were alone in the container.

However, Ester came back very quickly and she told me he had just given her a warning. I began to explain to her what he had done to me and she was horrified. On the outside I looked fine, because many of my bruises were under my clothes.

Another guard, whose name was Dawit, came and told us to go into our container to eat, then to come straight back out. But the heat of the sun had made my injuries swell, and I was unable to stand. I staggered a few steps and collapsed. He shouted, 'Why are you sleeping? Get up!'

'Please, Dawit,' I said, 'I am really sick. Just let me lie here.' But he didn't believe me, and kicked me to try to make me get up. When I couldn't he dragged me into the container. I just lay where he had left me, and Ester brought a wet cloth to bathe my wounds.

In what seemed like no time at all, Dawit came back, but we had not eaten, so Ester begged him for more time. But I could not even think about eating, because I was sure that I was dying.

I started to repeat the words of an old hymn over and over in my head, 'Lord be with me, Lord be with me, Lord be with me.' Tears ran down my cheeks as I thought of my family and my daughter coming to visit, only to be told by the guards that I was dead. I was not afraid to die, but I did not want to leave Eva.

Ester was still shouting at Dawit, and he hit her and pushed her out of the container. He dragged me out, and Ester pulled on his arm, saying, 'She is in pain. How can you do this to her?'

I didn't want her to end up in trouble, so I told her, 'It's over. I'm dying, so just forget him. You don't need to talk to him, because he won't be able to hurt me soon.' She just stared at me, because even now my injuries did not look as serious as they were.

He chained us both again in the sun, but I could not manage to sit upright and I collapsed again. 'I am dying, Ester,' I repeated, and I saw that at last she believed me.

'What can I do for you?' she asked, beginning to cry.

I said, 'Tell Dawit to take my chains off, so I can have a comfortable death.'

A small group of guards had started to collect beside us, and one of the older, kindly guards came to kneel beside me. 'Helen, what do you want us to do?' he asked, gently.

I whispered, 'Release my hands,' and then the world faded into darkness.

10

'What Has He Done to You?'

I found out later what had happened next. The older guard had said, 'Helen is gone,' and Ester had started to scream hysterically, until her voice had given out. Dawit had told the other guards that he didn't know I had been tortured. Obviously very worried that he would get into trouble if I died, he'd kept shouting my name and pouring water over me to try to revive me.

I had just fainted. When I regained consciousness I was soaking wet and surrounded by guards. Everyone shouted, 'She has come back to life!' and they called one of the medics. When the medic came he tried to lift me, but it was so painful that I nearly fainted again. Poor Ester screamed at them all to leave me alone.

There was a small clinic in one of the mud huts I had thought were toilets when I first arrived. It had three beds and some very basic facilities, and they carried me there. When they laid me in the bed, I felt as though there was something constricting my throat and stopping my breathing, so I kept trying to sit up. The medic thought at first that I was suffering from hunger, until he was told that I had been beaten. He asked everyone to leave, and he undressed me. But it appeared as though I was still dressed, because by now my whole body had gone black with bruises. He was shocked, and said, 'Helen, what has he done to you? What kind of stick or whip did he use?'

When I told him how Suleiman had beaten me, the medic went outside the door and cried. When he came back, he said, 'Why did you let him do this? You should have screamed. Do you realize you may never be able to walk again? I will help you as much as I can, but you will have great problems in the future, Helen.' He pointed out my injuries – my legs and shoulder were swollen, my thighs were bleeding, and so were the wounds at the back of my neck.

He called Suleiman to the clinic, and when he came the medic pointed to my neck, saying, 'You have probably damaged something here. She could die.' He showed him my legs as well, and said, 'Look at this. There is so much damage. She needs to be treated in hospital.'

But Suleiman refused to let me go, as he wanted to hide what he had done. So when he had gone, the medic put me on an IV drip. Then he began to massage my wounds. One of the interrogators came in as he was doing this, and when he saw my wounds he ran back out. The medic called him back to help, and together they cleaned my body with iodine solution. The smell stung my nostrils and the pain of the iodine competed with the burning all over my body. The interrogator had to hold me down so that the medic could work.

They still thought that I should eat, so they brought me some soft food: yoghurt and injera (the flat bread eaten with most meals in Eritrea). But every time I tried to swallow I felt like I was going to be sick, so I begged them to stop and just let me rest.

When they had left me to sleep, another prisoner came to the clinic for emergency treatment because he had cut his hand. I had been teaching him and he was now a strong believer. I had some more teachings hidden in a zipped pocket in my underwear, and I wanted to give them to him. But I was lying on my back with the medic between our two beds, and I couldn't get the papers out. I was surprised that I could still be worrying about this when I was so seriously ill, and I did wonder what Suleiman would think if he caught me passing these teachings on, after all he had just done to me.

As I lay there, it began to rain, and I heard a rumbling from outside. I could not sit up to look, but I knew that it was probably bricks collapsing in one of the poorly constructed mud brick buildings. I hoped that the clinic would hold together while I lay there.

It was late at night when they carried me back to my container, while the other prisoners were sleeping. I spent the whole night in severe pain, and I kept asking Ester to call the guard so that I could die in the fresh air. I continually felt that something was cutting off my breath – it turned out that it was the swelling from my injuries constricting my throat. Whenever Ester called for help a medic came and gave me an injection of painkillers, but it seemed to make no difference to me.

For days I lay in my container, mostly sleepless with the pain. I managed to eat a little lentil soup, but mostly I had no appetite. I thought a lot about what had happened, and about how cruel humans could be to each other. Yet I could not hate Suleiman. He had beaten me in anger, and I wondered if now he was ashamed. I did not want him to be punished for what he had done to me, but I prayed that one day he would find the faith in the Lord that I had, and come to repent of what he had done.

I asked for Suleiman to visit me, and he came to the container because he thought that I had changed my mind after my beating and was willing to sign the paper. He asked me how my wounds were, and was astonished when I said that I was fine. When he asked what I wanted, I told him, 'I cannot sleep. I am in constant pain, and I feel as though I cannot breathe. If I have to die, I want to see my daughter before I do. Please let me see her.'

'It is better, Helen,' he said, 'for you to ask to be released rather than have your daughter visit you here. You know what you have to do, and then I will release you. Sometimes I think that you cannot be human. You must be made of metal, because nothing seems to affect you.'

Then he spoke to me in a softer voice. 'Why not just ask to be released? You have done enough for your faith; you are nearly dead anyway. It will count as if you had died. So you have done your job, and you can give your faith up and die at home.' But again I refused, and so he would not let me see Eva.

During this time I was so grateful to God for my friend Ester. She served me tirelessly, and it is because of her care that I am still able to walk. She massaged and bathed me daily, fed me and washed my clothes, but never complained. Despite her care, though, my health deteriorated and I was bleeding non-stop. My legs were always swollen.

While I was still suffering, one of the Muslim guards came to beat us again. We suspected that Suleiman had sent him, because I had defied him again when I refused to ask for my release. The guard ordered us to lie flat so that he could beat us with a stick.

Ester was angry. 'Why are you doing this? Don't you know Helen is still being treated for serious injuries? I don't care if you want to beat me, but you should not beat her at all.'

But he obviously already knew that I was injured, because he did not reply. When he struck my wounds the pain was unbearable.

My screams and Ester's entreaties brought one of the medics running. 'You should not beat her! If she dies, it is not my responsibility.'

The medics are supposed to keep prisoners alive when they have been tortured, and they work very hard to do this. Often they are punished if a prisoner dies.

My legs were so damaged that I could not walk to the toilet. I found it humiliating to use the toilet bucket in front of the other prisoners who now shared our container, so I started to ask for sanitary towels. I used all the prison's supplies, and then they gave me bandages from the clinic. There were no female staff there, so I had to ask for everything from the male prison officers, which is embarrassing for a woman in my culture. So Ester began to carry me on

her back to the toilet. I had been known in prison for jog-
ging on the spot in the container, in my trainers, but now
everyone was very shocked to see me like this, and felt
sorry for me – even some of the guards. When I refused to
use the bucket or to eat, Ester insisted. I told her that if I
ate I would need the toilet, so I preferred just to drink. It
affected me psychologically – being in a locked container,
unable to walk, humiliated by the toilet facilities, and crippled with severe pain.

Another medic was called one day because of the bad
swelling in my legs, and he asked what had happened.
When I explained, he said that they should have taken me
to hospital there and then. But there was nothing I could
do; I was helpless and getting worse. There were three
medics at the prison, and each of them recommended that
I should be sent to hospital, but Suleiman would not allow
it.

Around this time I read *The Heavenly Man* by Brother
Yun, which someone had translated into my language,
Tigrinya, and smuggled into prison, and I was encouraged
and comforted by what I read. I still continued to write to
prisoners. The guards came every now and then to check
my health, but I wrote under my blanket so they would not
see. Ester distributed my letters on the way to the toilet in
the morning, and we changed our tactics all the time to
avoid detection, sometimes bundling them up in cloth, or
Ester would tuck them into her clothes.

However, one day I hadn't finished a letter so Ester waited for me. I had just given it to her when Suleiman came
into the container. She covered it quickly with a blanket,

but he saw, and he collected up all my papers and took them to his office. Ester went to the toilet, and while she was away, he came back.

'You are still writing, Helen? In this letter it says, "Sorry it has been a while since I wrote to you, but I have many sheep to write to, so I gave priority to those in the worst situation." What does that mean?'

The person whose letter that was had seemed to be doing well, and I thought he didn't need much teaching or encouragement, while many others were depressed. I did have lots of sheep to write to; some were believers, so I would send them Bible studies for discussion, and they sent comments and questions back, but I also wrote to non-believers to share my faith and to encourage them. Many prisoners had tried to commit suicide, so I sent them messages of hope. I also communicated with some of the prison guards, and some began to read the Bible. Of course, I did not tell Suleiman any of this.

Suleiman said, 'I give up on you, Helen.'

I told him that I would not stop, and he knew after all they had subjected me to that I meant it. Instead, he asked me for the names of the people that I wrote to, so that he could give them 'advice', because I had used code names on the letters.

'If I forsake my sheep for the enemy, I am not a shepherd,' I said. 'I must protect them.'

He stared at me. 'What are these sheep? When you say you are busy sending letters to other sheep, do you mean you are still teaching? You are locked in this container, how can you complain of being busy?' He lost his temper again and declared, 'It is no problem, though, because I am going to hang you!' He went back to his office, saying, 'I have done with you. I will not waste my time talking to you again.'

He meant what he said, because he assigned me to another interrogator. When I was first arrested I had met this man, whose name was Daniel, but he had not been there for many months so he did not know about my torture. He must have been away training because when he came back he was made chief interrogator.

The guards carried me to Daniel because I could not walk. I sat in his office and watched as he started to pace around; the way he did this, I could see he was putting on a show, trying to frighten or impress me with the importance of his new position. At last he said, 'Helen, everyone reads their Bible. I have two Bibles. Do you want me to show you?'

I knew that he was acting, and I laughed inside. We have a saying in Eritrea: 'A new broom cleans everything.' He didn't know that even Suleiman had given up on me, so he was trying hard to intimidate me. He brought the police baton over and put it on the desk in front of me. 'Helen, I'm warning you. Stop believing or I will beat you with this.'

I looked at him and I laughed. 'Are you trying to scare me with this baton? This baton is not new to me! I have been beaten with it until I was nearly dead. I still did not change my mind. So if you want to beat me you can, but unless God wills it, you cannot kill me.'

He looked taken aback, and said, 'OK . . . But I want the name of the person you wrote this letter to. I already know who it is, but I want to hear it from you.'

'If you already know, then why ask me?' I said.

Some of his staff members had degrees and were always suspected because they had an education. He named one of them, but I just replied, 'I have never given away any names, and I never will.'

He changed his tack, and began to speak gently to me. 'Helen, they don't care for you, these people you write to. Look at how you were, and how you are now. Your body is deteriorating. Don't you have any concern for your own health?'

But I would not be persuaded, and so he sent me back to my container.

When I got back to the container, I began to feel worse, so I called for the medic. I told him, 'I'm losing a lot of blood and I feel dizzy. Can't you stop the bleeding?'

He gave me an injection, which made me feel numb. I thought perhaps it might be a sedative, but when I asked him what it was, he said, 'We don't have any medicine to treat you, so I'm just trying what we have.'

'You are treating me like a guinea pig!' I said.

Ester looked at the ampoule and saw that it had expired a long time ago, but when she told the medic this, he just laughed. 'Aren't you two the experts! I told you, we don't have any more medicine.'

Because my injuries had not received proper treatment, my condition deteriorated until I could no longer urinate, and I couldn't even stand, let alone walk. The guards brought a stretcher to the container and carried me on it to the clinic. The medic called Suleiman and Daniel, the chief interrogator, and told them firmly, 'Her body is shutting down and her health is now very poor. If we leave her here, she will die.'

Suleiman shook his head. 'She is fine. Hunger is her main problem; she will get better if we feed her.'

Ester had come with me and now she was unable to contain herself. 'Hunger!' she shouted at the surprised men. 'How dare you say that! That is just an excuse. Helen is sick because you tortured her!' They stared at her for a moment, then turned back to the medic as though she wasn't there, and began to give instructions for food to be brought.

When the food arrived, Daniel forced my mouth open while Suleiman spooned lentil soup into it as though I were a baby. I found their actions offensive, because I knew that they were just pretending to be concerned about me. I kept telling them, 'Please, stop. I do not want to eat. I am happy with just the IV drip.'

Suleiman and Daniel decided to keep me in the clinic, and they allowed Ester to stay so that she could carry me to the toilet field in the night. They assigned a guard to us. As I said, the clinic was in one of the mud brick buildings, and it was almost as basic as the container. There were just three beds there with thin mattresses, a few basic medical supplies, and a bare light bulb hanging from the roof, which was made of two layers of corrugated iron and was full of holes. The worst thing was that the clinic was infested with rats – I could see them clambering around above me. That first night, the medic had no sooner switched the light off than I felt something pulling at my sleeve. There was a rat on the bed with me, pulling at my clothes with its sharp little teeth. From then on I kept the light on every night to try to discourage them, and I always had one of my cats with me; but the rats were very determined. Unsurprisingly, I found it hard to sleep.

My condition continued to worsen, and finally Suleiman allowed the medic to take me to hospital. The guards brought a truck round and Ester carried me to it. It was 2006, and I had been in prison for thirty-one months and two weeks. Ester is still in prison.

11

Release

As the truck rolled out of the prison, I was in too much pain to feel truly relieved. However, as we entered the city again I started to look around. It helped to distract me from the jolts of pain as the truck rumbled along the streets. I had not seen the city in over two years, and I had missed it. After all this time, the city looked older, too, more haggard and careworn. Like me, it had deteriorated.

The truck pulled up at the hospital, and one of the guards went in and brought out a wheelchair. They lifted me into it and wheeled me inside. Feeling a little sick, I asked the nurses to take me to the toilet, and on the way I caught sight of a Christian doctor I had known before my arrest. I knew that he, too, had been imprisoned, but I was shocked to see him. His hair had gone grey and his face was covered with blotchy discolorations. They are caused by hormone changes which are usually seen in pregnant women, but in his case they were due to stress. He was also in hospital receiving treatment, and he was surrounded by prison guards. He looked shocked to see me, too.

This was the first time I had seen a proper doctor since I had been arrested. The medics in prison are really first-aiders, and not qualified medical professionals. When I explained to my doctor that my condition was due to torture, his expression darkened.

'I will make sure that you are admitted as a patient. They cannot send you back to prison in this state.'

My mother was a nurse at this hospital, and someone had called her to let her know that I was there. She came in from her work with another patient, and when I saw her I burst into tears. I was so relieved to see her, but I couldn't believe how much older she looked. She tried to control her shock at my condition, but I knew that she was horrified.

The guards who had brought me to hospital were standing at the door to my room, and one of them said, 'Helen, you are human after all. We have never seen you cry before.'

When, after a few days, I was allowed visitors, my whole family came. A nurse pushed me on a wheelchair to meet them. Everyone cried and wailed when they saw me, especially my grandmother and Eva. Eva was almost hysterical. She kept crying, 'My mother is paralysed! Will she never be able to walk again?' No one could answer her, because my condition was so serious.

I was happy to be in hospital, though, because at last I was getting proper medical care and I could once again have food brought to me by my family, which supplemented the hospital diet. Sadly, my friend the Christian doctor could not enjoy such home-cooked food. Prisoners being treated in hospital were given food twice a day, and were not usually allowed to receive anything from visitors – although they made an exception in my case, perhaps because I was so ill and had been beaten so badly. At mealtimes, a woman would carry a huge pan into the ward. It was usually pasta (which is popular in Eritrea because of our Italian colonizers), but overcooked as though it were porridge, and served plain, without sauce. My doctor friend was very ill with diabetes, liver problems and asthma from his time in prison, and he needed good food, but this was all he received. He had been a respected doctor from a good family, but he would line up meekly with the other prisoners. One day I watched as the woman scooped a lump of mushy pasta from the big pan and slapped it onto his plate. I sat in my wheelchair outside in the fresh air and the sun, and I cried. How unhappy I was to see my friend suffer in this way! This man had helped so many people and he had done nothing wrong. He was imprisoned because of his faith, and now he was being punished for the simple crime of believing in Jesus.

Later that day I watched him trying to wash his clothes, as they make the prisoners do that themselves. As was usual, his family had always employed a maid to do this, and my poor friend was not doing a very good job. In Eritrea, boys never do the washing. Sometimes even the girls don't, if there is a maid to do it. I tried to lighten the mood and asked teasingly, 'Are you enjoying your washing?'

He turned to me with a rueful smile, and said, 'Helen, I've never even washed a handkerchief before.'

The hospital sent word to the prison that my health was too poor to allow me to go back. They had settled me in a room for female prisoners, but I was on my own as there were no other women there at the time. Across the corridor was a male prisoners' ward. Whenever someone died they would put him on a stretcher and leave him in the corridor in front of my door. I saw dead bodies all the time. Gradually, I began to feel that everyone who came to hospital died. Of course, this was not the case. It was just that these prisoners were only brought to hospital from prison when they were dying and it was usually too late for the doctors to save them. But I started to become paranoid and I suspected that the doctors were killing them on purpose. When they tried to give me medicine I was afraid that they would do the same to me. My heart was filled with dark thoughts and doubt, even though I was a Christian.

I had no privacy. I was pushed to the toilet in a wheelchair and had to be helped to bathe – and there were still guards at the hospital.

The doctors started to give me injections for the pain but then had to change to paracetamol as these injections were bad for my liver. The paracetamol was not as effective, and I often needed to call for the nurse in the night because the pain was so severe. Eventually, I became reluctant to call the doctors and nurses from their sleep. My left leg still did not improve – it kept swelling, and whenever I put my foot to the floor, I felt a severe shooting pain.

The doctors were keen to help me to walk again, but I found it hard because of my left leg, and it was too soon for physiotherapy. They wanted to transfer me to the specialist hospital at Oreta, on the other side of Asmara. Instead, my parents suggested that the hospital release me into their care and they would register me at Oreta as an outpatient.

My parents brought me home. They started to feed me properly, inject me and bathe me. My father took me to Oreta regularly for treatment, and I began to improve steadily. However, although I had officially been released from prison, I was always under surveillance. The house was surrounded by secret police. They were always stopping my parents and asking, 'How is Helen's leg? Is she improving?' Even when visitors came, I found it difficult to talk because I was afraid they might report to the secret police. I knew that if they should feel I had improved sufficiently, there was a good chance they would take me back to prison, where I would surely die.

So I made secret plans to leave Eritrea. I went to the Sudanese Embassy and begged for a visa to enter Sudan. It was a miracle that I got the visas, because if the authorities had known that I was planning to leave, they would have stopped me. Although they followed me everywhere, they seemed blind to what I was actually doing, and I felt the hand of God on my situation.

I went to have a medical check-up and the doctor asked, 'Why do you need this particular check-up? This is the one that you have just before you leave the country.'

I said, 'I just need a check-up.'

He shrugged, and carried it out.

There was a one in a hundred chance that I would be able to leave Eritrea by plane. Most people have to escape over the border, but I was crippled and would not have made it. It felt as though God had been directing everything – my release from prison, then my release from hospital, and now all these events leading to my escape from Eritrea.

At the airport I was waiting to check in, supported by my crutches, and I saw one security guard staring at me. I was afraid that he somehow knew who I was and what I was doing. He walked over to me and I felt my legs becoming shaky, but then he put a hand on my arm to steady me.

'Let me help you,' he said.

I murmured my thanks, and he smiled. 'We must help those who fought so bravely for our country.'

He thought that I had been handicapped in the war with Ethiopia, although I had given no indication that he was correct. When I handed my passport over they barely glanced at it; my picture was an older one and the names 'Helen' and 'Berhane' are common in Eritrea. I felt as though God was blinding the people who might have stopped me.

On the plane they put me in a seat reserved for the disabled, by the window. As we took off, I looked out of the window and saw Asmara spread out below me. I screwed up my eyes against the sun and in the distance, I thought I glimpsed the prison where I had spent more than two years suffering for my God. I could barely believe that now I was leaving my beloved country. I felt as though any moment I would wake up on the cold, hard floor of my container, to find that my freedom was just a dream.

But it was real, and by God's grace I was free.

12

Freedom

Although I had left Eritrea behind, my journey had only just begun. My elder sister met me at the airport in Sudan and took me to her home. I found it hard to adjust to life there, at first. Sudan is hotter than Eritrea, and I spent most of the day alone while my sister went to her job in an internet café. I started to see a doctor regularly; my treatment was expensive, but my family and friends in Eritrea, and many more through the Christian organization Release Eritrea, were helping to support me. I was especially amazed to discover that people I had never met had been praying for me while I was in captivity, and I was grateful for their prayers.

I still took six different types of medication daily, but with good food and freedom I was improving. I had suffered from memory loss after my beating, but now my memory seemed to be coming back. The doctor in Sudan told me that the muscles in my left leg had wasted, and that he could see when he scanned me on ultrasound that I had liver damage, so he treated me for that as well.

He recommended that I exercise to build up my strength, so an old friend from church who now lived in Sudan came to take me to the gym every day. When I first started it was difficult because it hurt to even stand, and I often lost my balance, but over time I improved.

However, I was still not safe. Most days the phone would ring and when I answered it, I would hear a voice saying, 'We are watching you.' I was also worried about Eva, who had stayed in Eritrea with my parents. I was afraid that if she stayed then I would never see her again, or the government might try to hurt her. I also knew that when she reached 17 she would have to join the military, and I wanted a better future for my daughter. The secret police were still watching me, and there was no chance that Eva would be able to leave the country the way I did. So I made the difficult decision to have her smuggled out of Eritrea.

There was a man who took people out across the border, so I made contact with him, and paid him to take Eva from Asmara and across the desert into Sudan. I knew how dangerous it was; many traffickers lead their group into the desert, rob them and leave them to die, and even if the man was honourable they could still be caught. Also, it was a long and dangerous journey for a girl of 12 to make. But I believed in my heart that it was Eva's only chance for a better life. Before I left Eritrea I had sent someone to visit the family of my good friend Elsa who I had shared a container with, who had been sent to spy on me and who I had come to love like a sister, to see if they had any news of her. But they had heard nothing. I knew that our other friend Rahel had been released, but I couldn't find out where she was, and when I sent someone to visit her family they were reluctant to talk, as they were afraid that the government would put her back in prison if they heard that I had been trying to make contact with her. So I knew that I could not leave Eva in Eritrea, as it seemed that the government was determined to find ways to punish me through those I loved.

I sat in Khartoum and prayed, while my daughter was driven through the night in a jeep with no lights, to ensure they could not be seen. The trafficker's son lay on the roof and hissed directions. The journey was long and hard. Food I had paid for never turned up and, at one point, when they had to walk for a time, Eva was so weak that one of the other refugees had to carry her on his back through the dust and the heat. Once over the border, she spent several days in a detention centre, where a girl in her group was believed to have been raped by a Sudanese security officer, and then in a refugee camp before my sister met her in Khartoum and brought her home. I thanked God that he had kept her safe, and I was grateful to the men who had smuggled her out.

I had already made plans for us to leave Sudan, because in the five months between leaving Eritrea and Eva joining me, I had been forced to move four times as the phone calls persisted. They got more threatening over time. When I asked who was calling, they would reply, 'You don't need my name. You will know me when I get you.' So there was a real danger that someone would come and kidnap or kill us.

Although I was not singing at churches in Sudan, an Eritrean pastor wanted me to do a gospel concert at his

church in Khartoum. Without telling me, he had posters
made with my picture on and distributed them around the
city. The Eritrean government heard about it, and I had to
move house immediately. Release Eritrea cancelled the
concert and tried to explain to the pastor how dangerous
this was for me, but he didn't understand what the government was capable of, and even quoted the Bible, 'Do not
be afraid.' He wanted to go ahead with the concert and
actually came to pick me up in a taxi, but I had already
moved. Release Eritrea were working hard to find us asylum in America or Europe. I didn't mind where we went. I
told them, 'We will take the first application that is successful,' which turned out to be Denmark.

When we landed in Copenhagen, it was like a different
world. We are both city girls, and we had never lived in a
small village before. To get to our new home we had to drive
a long way from Copenhagen, to a small community in the
countryside, beside the sea. It was strange for both of us.
When I first arrived I was almost immobile, but as my condition improved I longed for the noise and bustle of Asmara.
It was especially hard for Eva, because we had moved into an
elderly community and there was nowhere to go to meet
young people. She was used to living with my parents and my
younger sister, and now it was just the two of us. There was
no school – we discovered that Eva would have to travel each
day to the nearest town. When I was well enough, I began to
go there once a week to the language school to learn Danish
and English.

But for us, Denmark has so many positive things. At
home I got nothing but imprisonment, beatings and abuse,

but although the Danish people are not my people, they have looked after me as though I was one of their own.

In Denmark I receive treatment for my eyesight, which is now poor. I have problems with my teeth because of the prison food but now I have proper dental care. Once a week there are two ladies who come to clean the house and do the laundry for both of us. Every time I think of the kindness of the Danish government and their people I pray that God will bless them.

The populations of Denmark and Eritrea are almost the same size, but in Denmark I can see that the people respect and appreciate each other. Everyone works for their country's development and progress. In Denmark they not only care about human rights, they also care for the rights of animals! I will always envy them and wish that the same was true of my country. If anyone is hard-working in Eritrea, the government does not appreciate it. They stop you working for your country, as they stopped me. It is clear that the Danish government is committed to helping their people – all their activities are focused on improving and expanding things like healthcare and education. But in Eritrea it is quite the opposite; the government spends its time expanding prisons but doesn't work for the benefit of the people. This is why so many of us are exiled. I feel ashamed when I think of it; we have enough land, and we could feed our own people. Yet Denmark is not only supporting its own but also taking care of thousands of refugees. I truly value the freedom I have here to follow and preach my faith.

When I was well enough to walk with two sticks, I started my spiritual ministry again – singing. I started to attend Bible studies, and ministered in churches nearby. Now I have improved so much I can walk slowly without a stick, and I have started to minister in other countries: Holland, Germany and Sweden. In the future I pray I will be able to travel all over the world to spread the gospel. I thank God that I sleep well and have not suffered any lasting psychological trauma from my   experiences, as so many victims of torture do. I have truly experienced in life what I read in the Bible in Paul's second letter to the Corinthians – the external body may be destroyed but the inner is renewed day by day. Above all, I have no fear. I can go out and return to my house safely. When I was in prison, everything was controlled – when to eat, when to sleep, even when to go to the toilet, but now I am free to take a bath at whatever time of day I want. It is my prayer for all those who are still suffering in prisons that they, too, will have the freedom I enjoy.

My new life in Denmark is entirely through God's grace, and I live for my Lord. If he should choose to send me elsewhere I will go and be happy. In prison I learned that human beings need so little to survive, so now I am not afraid of anything the future might bring. I cannot work in Denmark at the moment, and I have very limited resources, but I am satisfied with what I have. I have learnt to be content even in small places, and to thank God in spite of hardships. Although humans are limited in what they can do, God is unlimited. He was with me in prison, he was with me in Sudan, he is with me in Denmark, and I know he will be with me wherever I may go.

Epilogue

I never dreamed I would leave my country, but most Eritrean Christians are forced to leave because of our faith: we have no freedom to read the book we love or to worship our God. A lot of intellectuals and educated people have also had to leave, yet Eritrea needs them if it is to develop and prosper. All of us are forced to shake the dust of our land from our feet, and we have found that it is true that a prophet is not respected in their own country. All we got in Eritrea was degradation and humiliation. We were tortured, we offered our backs to their sticks and batons, and we were separated from those we loved.

My prayer is for all this to change and God to bring the persecution in Eritrea to an end. Many pastors spend their lives in prison, their children are orphaned and never know their parents; a bride is separated from her groom; and families and friends are dispersed all over the world. I want to encourage every Christian to pray for these things to come to an end. My wish is simple: To live like other people, peacefully in my country. I pray daily that Eritrea will one day be a place where the gospel can be preached freely and that my country will be a blessing for all nations.

So I want to give a message to those of you who are Christians and live in the free world: you must not take your freedom for granted. Use every opportunity to praise the Lord every day. If I could sing in prison, imagine what you can do for God's glory with your freedom.

I also have a message for my tormentors. I want to tell them that I love them and that I hope one day they will believe in the Jesus that I serve.

I want to remind the Eritrean government that we speak the same language, we have the same origins and we are the same colour. We are all people of Eritrea, yet the government persecutes us for our beliefs. I invite them to change, to choose love instead of hatred, to spread harmony among the people. The authorities must learn to be tolerant and loving, to work towards progress and development, and to build rather than destroy.

I want to leave you with the words of a song I wrote in prison.

> Our father Abraham travelled three days to sacrifice
>   his son
> From Philistia to the land of Moriah.
> That place witnessed Abraham's reward.
> He had no regrets on his first day,
> No regrets on the second day,
> And no regrets on the third day.
> His determination was amazing,
> The trip to Moriah was extraordinary.

God still has faithful followers,
Promise-keepers who stand firm on his Word.
The God of Abraham is faithful,
He is faithful enough to keep his word.

CHORUS: Christianity costs you your life
But at the end, its outcome is victory.

Faithful servants who refused to be persuaded by
   the king's reward
Resolved not to defile themselves with the king's food.
They looked better nourished than all the other
   young men
And were able to stand before the kings.

CHORUS: Christianity costs you your life
But at the end, its outcome is victory.

The beating of the Hebrews with the whip was awful.
The waves of the sea and the mighty wind
Crushed by the stone, suffering by day and by night;
Paul's faithfulness was tested by a sword.

CHORUS: Christianity costs you your life
But at the end, its outcome is victory.

The journey of Ruth was a hope where there was
   no hope;
A sacrifice was paid even for a despised tribe.
Although there was nothing promised for Ruth

By faith she made her way towards Nazareth
And she entered into Jesus' genealogy.

CHORUS: Christianity costs you your life
But at the end, its outcome is victory.

Above all, I dream that one day I will return to my beloved
country, and that I will sing a song of praise in the stadium
in Asmara. With God, all things are possible, and so I pray
that one day, it may be so.

Further Information

Release Eritrea

Release Eritrea is a human rights organization founded in 2004 by a group of Eritreans living in the UK, to promote religious tolerance among Eritreans, and support and act as advocates on behalf of those who, like Helen Berhane, have become victims of religious persecution.

Release Eritrea lobbies internationally to ensure that policy-makers keep the issues of religious tolerance in Eritrea on their agenda; it offers assistance to those who have been victims of religious persecution whilst they are within the country and whilst living as refugees and asylum seekers elsewhere, works with Eritrean faith groups, civic and political organizations to promote religious tolerance among Eritreans, and organizes prayer and intercession events to offer prayers on behalf of victims of religious persecution. For more information, please visit www.release-eritrea.org.uk.

Helen Berhane's book, *Song of the Nightingale*, is a timely addition to Western Christian bookshops. While newspapers continue to carry accounts of what is termed the 'persecution' of Christians in the West, *Song of the Nightingale* brings to our attention the actual, exceptionally brutal persecution of the Church in other parts of the world.

Helen's story begins in her native Eritrea – a country of five million people that borders Sudan and Ethiopia. Early on, readers learn that Helen is a successful businesswoman, single mother, vocalist and committed follower of Christ. It is from this life that she is taken and imprisoned for sharing her faith in Jesus.

The book follows Helen's story of determination as she refuses to renounce her faith despite horrific cruelties inflicted on her. It is a story that won't fail to grip, infuriate, disturb and break the heart of the reader. However, what makes the story so gripping is how it illustrated the way God refines his people by fire. The beauty of Helen's relationship with Christ shines through all the tortures inflicted by her captors by virtue of her response to them and to other prisoners.

Her final challenge at the end of the book is one we in the West should take to heart: 'To those of you who are Christians and live in the free world: You must not take your freedom for granted . . . If I could sing in prison, imagine what you can do for God's glory with your freedom.'

The Salvationist, September 2010

This is a remarkable book in which Helen Berhane tells her own story of persecution, imprisonment and torture in her native Eritrea. She was eventually released and sent to hospital due to severe ill-health, and then she escaped to Sudan, from where she went to live in Denmark. The narrative is pacey and gripping as the story moves from Berhane's simple childhood into the dramatic show of strength between, on the one hand, her determined faith and willingness to suffer and, on the other hand, the brutal oppression of the Eritrean regime.

Berhane was not a fluent English speaker at the time of writing, but the text reads well and the narrative is clear. There is something particularly powerful in telling such a dramatic story without any sense of embellishment or over-emphasis. Part of the purpose of the book is to highlight the oppressive nature of the Eritrean regime and in this respect the book is a success. I strongly recommend it.

Martin Charlesworth, *Christianity Magazine*,
August 30, 2012

Authentic

We trust you enjoyed reading this book from Authentic. If you want to be informed of any new titles from this author and other releases you can sign up to the Authentic newsletter by scanning below:

Online:
authenticmedia.co.uk

Follow us: